OECD Studies on SMEs and Entrepreneurship

SME Policy in Czechia

OECD
BETTER POLICIES FOR BETTER LIVES

Please cite this publication as:
OECD (2026), *SME Policy in Czechia*, OECD Studies on SMEs and Entrepreneurship, OECD Publishing, Paris, https://doi.org/10.1787/73cde8ec-en.

ISBN 978-92-64-79596-9 (print)
ISBN 978-92-64-99584-0 (PDF)
ISBN 978-92-64-64923-1 (HTML)

OECD Studies on SMEs and Entrepreneurship
ISSN 2078-0982 (print)
ISSN 2078-0990 (online)

Photo credits: Cover © TomasSereda/Getty Images Plus.

Corrigenda to OECD publications may be found at: https://www.oecd.org/en/publications/support/corrigenda.html.

Foreword

This publication is the main outcome of the project "Mid-term evaluation of the Czech SME Support Strategy 2021-2027", undertaken by the OECD Centre for Entrepreneurship, SMEs, Regions and Cities in collaboration with the Czech Ministry of Industry and Trade (MIT) and with financial support from the Reform and Investment Task Force of the European Commission (SG REFORM). The project also led to the development of a detailed Action Plan comprising more than twenty targeted policy actions, delivered to the Czech MIT and SG REFORM.

The project was conducted between July 2024 and July 2025. The methodology combined desk-based analysis with a one-week fact-finding mission, during which the OECD Secretariat conducted structured consultations with government and non-government stakeholders involved in SME policy. The analytical process was complemented by a final technical workshop, which served to validate findings and policy conclusions with the same stakeholders.

The report consists of seven thematic chapters, which closely reflects the areas addressed by the government's "Strategy to Support Small and Medium-Sized Enterprises in the Czech Republic, 2021-2027": i) business environment; ii) SME financing; iii) SME internationalisation; iv) SME skills development and entrepreneurship skills; v) SME R&D and innovation; vi) SME digitalisation; vii) the green transition of SMEs. Each chapter follows the same structure and includes: i) a short baseline assessment of SME conditions in Czechia; ii) an in-depth evaluation of recent policy trends; iii) targeted policy recommendations meant to inspire national SME policy making in the short-to-medium term.

The report shows that recent government reforms have significantly simplified administrative and tax procedures in Czechia, notably through digitalisation and the introduction of a flat-tax regime for sole traders. Nonetheless, administrative complexity remains a significant concern for many SMEs. Further reforms, such as streamlined insolvency procedures and an easier VAT registration process, could give an additional boost to the simplification agenda of the government.

The report also underscores that there is scope for improving access to finance for Czech SMEs, both through traditional tools like credit guarantees and stronger development of the domestic VC market, and for increasing the number of Czech SMEs engaged in international markets, such as through the launch of a revamped national supplier development programme.

The report finally recognises that the Czech government has made important advances in the twin transition of SMEs, fostering their digital and green transformation through a suite of mostly EU-funded programmes. In this respect, Czechia's digital innovation hubs appear to work well, but they will need stable funding to have a long-term impact on the digital competencies of Czech SMEs. "Green" programmes have covered many different areas, including energy efficiency, renewable energy adoption, and the circular economy. Going forward, it will be important to reform the national energy audit system and secure funding for "green" programmes also after the end of the national recovery and resilience fund, which has been the main source of funding.

This report contributes to the Programme of Work and Budget of the OECD Committee on SMEs and Entrepreneurship (CSMEE). It was submitted for comments via written procedure to the OECD CSMEE [CFE/SME(2025)10] on 10 April 2025.

Acknowledgements

The project behind this report was funded by the European Union via the Technical Support Instrument, and implemented by the OECD, in co-operation with the European Commission. This report was prepared by the OECD Centre for Entrepreneurship, SMEs, Regions and Cities, led by Lamia Kamal-Chaoui (Director), under the aegis of the OECD Committee on SMEs and Entrepreneurship (CSMEE). Marco Marchese (Policy Analyst) co-ordinated the project and provided oversight of the individual chapters. Lucia Cusmano (Head of the SME and Entrepreneurship Division) offered overall guidance and supervision of the project. The main authors of the report are Marco Marchese, Alexandra Rusu (Economist), Jan-Philipp Schmidt (Policy Analyst), and Maria Sobron Bernal (Policy Analyst), all from the OECD Centre for Entrepreneurship, SMEs, Regions and Cities, and Kris Boschmans (external expert).

The report would not have been possible without the active engagement of the Czech Ministry of Industry and Trade (MIT), which was the main counterpart of the OECD within the national government, and the Reform and Investment Task Force of the European Commission (SG REFORM). In particular, the OECD would like to thank Veronika Spirkova and Elina Lunova, both experts in SME development at the Czech MIT, for supporting the project throughout its steps, including the organisation of the fact-finding mission, the collection of background documents and comments from different government entities on the first draft report, and the organisation of the final technical workshop to disseminate the findings. The OECD also extends its gratitude to Martha Cambas, policy officer in SG REFORM, who closely followed the implementation of the project in the European Commission and ensured that the project's compliance with SG REFORM's guidelines.

The OECD also appreciates the participation in meetings and the comments received from different ministries, national agencies and other stakeholders, including the Association for the Capital Market of the Czech Republic, the Association of Small and Medium-Sized Enterprises and Crafts of the Czech Republic, the Confederation of Employers' and Business Associations of the Czech Republic, the Czech Chamber of Commerce, the Czech Export Bank, the Czech National Bank, the Czech Statistical Office, CzechInvest, CzechTrade, the Czech Industrial Property Office, Czech representatives of the European Digital Innovation Hubs, the Export Guarantee and Insurance Corporation, the Ministry of Education, Youth and Sports, the Ministry of Environment, the Ministry of Finance, the Ministry of Foreign Affairs, the Ministry of Interior, the Ministry of Justice, the Ministry of Labour and Social Affairs, the Ministry of Regional Development, the Ministry of Industry and Trade, the National Development Bank, the National Pedagogical Institute of the Czech Republic, the Prague Innovation Institute, the Prague Stock Exchange, the Office of the Government of the Czech Republic, the Technology Agency of the Czech Republic, the Technology Centre Prague, and the Union of Czech Production Co-operatives.

Heather Mortimer-Charoy and Juan Mendez (CFE) provided project and administrative assistance and prepared the report for publication.

Table of contents

FIGURES

TABLES

BOXES

Executive summary

This report assesses the implementation of the "Strategy to Support Small and Medium-sized Enterprises in the Czech Republic, 2021-2027", released by the Czech Ministry of Industry and Trade (MIT) at the end of 2021 to guide SME policy during the 2021-2027 EU Programming Period. The Strategy focused on closing the productivity gap between SMEs and large companies through objectives across seven policy dimensions: business environment, access to finance, access to markets, workforce skills and education, R&D and innovation, digitalisation, and low-carbon economy and resource efficiency.

In 2024, the MIT launched an independent mid-term evaluation of the implementation of the Strategy to reflect the significantly changed economic context, as the initial Strategy design pre-dated both the Covid-19 crisis and the following energy crisis, which had resulted, among other things, in higher inflation and interest rates and disruptions in global supply chains.

This evaluation report, therefore, provides an in-depth assessment of Czech SME policies with a view to proposing policy reforms aimed at enhancing SME productivity and competitiveness, while strengthening their resilience and ability to adapt to the new imperatives of the digital and green transition. The evaluation follows the same priority areas identified in the original National SME Support Strategy of Czechia.

The business environment

Almost three-quarters (72%) of Czech enterprises consider the complexity of administrative procedures a major barrier to doing business in Czechia, compared with the OECD average of 66%. The Czech government has introduced simplification reforms in recent years, mostly involving the digitalisation of administrative processes such as business registration, trade licenses and building permits. The government has also reduced the number of professional activities for which a trade license is needed, making further strides in its simplification agenda. Possible additional reforms would include setting up a one-stop web portal to submit all business forms online, a streamlined VAT registration process, and simpler insolvency procedures.

The Czech government has also made tax compliance easier for businesses, especially for the self-employed. Since 2021, sole traders with an annual turnover below CZK 2 million (i.e., about EUR 80 000) can opt for a flat tax, which increases certainty about tax duties and eases compliance. Communication with tax authorities has also been increasingly digitised. Going forward, the government could consider simplifying taxation also for employer SMEs, with a view to lowering compliance costs for a larger segment of the SME population and supporting the transition from non-employer to employer status.

SME financing

Like most OECD countries, Czechia has recently experienced an increase in interest rates to tackle surging inflation, which has led many SMEs to either postpone investments or to use retained earnings to finance such investments. Against this backdrop, the offer of government-backed credit guarantees, which could have supported debt finance at a time of tight credit market conditions, has instead shrunk. One reported reason is that the national development bank, which is in charge with the management of this scheme, has also been tasked with the delivery of many targeted interventions in the national recovery and resilience plan, which has stretched its implementation capacity.

As to equity finance, venture capital investment is low in Czechia, which limits the growth potential of innovative start-ups and SMEs. While some funds-of-funds have been launched with EU financial and institutional backing, Czechia's VC market remains underdeveloped. Policy reforms such as tax incentives for equity investors, new regulations allowing pension funds to participate in the VC market, and a stronger role of the national development bank in this asset class would support the further development of the Czech VC market.

SME internationalisation

Czech SMEs increased their export volumes by approximately 30% between 2012 and 2022, much more than peers in most other EU countries. However, the number of exporters has not changed dramatically, thus suggesting that more could be done to enhance the export readiness of a larger group of SMEs. Czech SMEs with export potential also find it difficult to access high value-added segments of global value chains (GVCs), especially in highly competitive sectors such as automotive and machinery, which reduces their ability to contribute to national exports indirectly through participation in GVCs.

CzechTrade's initiatives, notably its growing network of export incubators, economic diplomacy projects, and sector-specific initiatives (e.g. the Design Centre), play a key role in supporting the export activities of Czech SMEs. Nevertheless, the sector and country coverage of some of these measures could be expanded, while underrepresented groups in business internationalisation (e.g. women entrepreneurs) could be better targeted through bespoke training and networking events. The offer of export finance (e.g., export credits and export guarantees) could also be scaled up, but it is currently constrained by the institutional setting governing the two public agencies charged with this mission. Finally, supplier development programmes, which have a strong tradition in Czechia (e.g., automotive industry) could be re-launched in emerging national sectors like electronics and semiconductors.

SME skills development and entrepreneurship skills

Fewer Czech adults than the EU average participate in training. While this is partly the result of a strong labour market, which makes the need for training less immediate, it may hinder the adaptation of the domestic workforce to new skills demands in the longer run. One of the mains skills policy priorities of the Czech government has been strengthening the digital skills of the workforce. The Czech government has also buttressed its offer of micro-credentials, which are short-term courses to address targeted skills needs. Micro-credentials are especially important at a time when skills profiles change rapidly due to the twin (digital and green) transition, and where this change often entails the development of new skills in existing jobs rather than the full development of new professional occupations.

Czechia's entrepreneurship ecosystem has expanded rapidly in the last decade, with an increased involvement of CzechInvest, the national investment agency, in start-up support. Nonetheless, the overall quality of the entrepreneurship ecosystem is heterogenous. For example, half of the existing business incubators/accelerators are not active, and another sizeable share only offers online/remote services. The offer of entrepreneurship education is also at an initial stage in Czechia, although there are some interesting initiatives both at secondary (e.g., "fictitious company" programme) and tertiary levels (e.g., Brno's regional innovation centre).

SME R&D and innovation

Czechia's innovation performance is close to the EU average, but business R&D spending remains relatively low, particularly among SMEs, which reduces the ability of the national business sector to introduce radical innovations. Czechia's Smart Specialisation Strategy sets out the main national innovation policy objectives and technology priority areas, which are closely followed by most government innovation programmes, regardless of the implementing ministry or agency. Public funding for R&D and innovation has also increased in recent years, although this is mostly due to external funding, especially from EU sources, rather than national funding.

Going forward, there is scope for streamlining the offer of government-funded innovation programmes, which is currently highly fragmented, although this might require merging some of the EU-funded national Operational Programmes. The national R&D tax credit policy, which is hardly used by Czech SMEs, could also be overhauled to make it more attractive for this business segment. In particular, the government could consider moving from a system where the tax base is corporate income to another where the tax base is payroll spending (e.g. for R&D-related personnel). This change would ease policy access for SMEs, especially those having no profits against which to claim a tax credit based on corporate income. Finally, Czechia could strengthen industry-university linkages by providing more stable funding for technology transfer offices and piloting industrial Ph.D. programmes.

SME digitalisation

Czechia has made notable progress in digitalisation, with 81% of companies having internet speed above 30 Mbit/s in 2023; however, access to high-speed broadband (100 Mbit/s) is still patchy. To drive the digital transformation, the Czech government has introduced a Strategic Plan for Digitalisation, while the national recovery and resilience plan has allocated EUR 662 million for supporting business digitalisation through different programmes.

The flagship initiative in this area is the network of six European Digital Innovation Hubs (EDIHs), which offer services related to digital skills and digital innovation to businesses, especially SMEs. Available evidence suggests that the EDIHs are functioning effectively. However, their longer-term impact is constrained by the current funding sunset clause in 2026. The government could also consider the development of additional hubs, potentially through a mixed-funding approach combining public and private resources.

The green transition of SMEs

Czechia has made important headways in the decarbonisation of the economy by improving energy efficiency and increasing the share of renewables in the national energy mix. However, it is still one of the most energy-intensive countries in the EU, which is a consequence of the comparatively heavier weight of manufacturing in the economy and wider use of coal in national electricity generation. Czech SMEs account for between 41-48% of business-sector greenhouse (GHG) emissions, in line with the EU average. However, only 14% of SMEs had a climate strategy in place in 2024, compared with 21% at the EU level.

The national government has actively encouraged energy efficiency, the uptake of renewable energy sources, and circular-economy practices by SMEs through a suite of programmes mostly funded by the national recovery and resilience plan, which will come to an end in 2026. Securing post-2026 funding for green programmes will, therefore, be one main challenge for the Czech government. The national energy audit system will also need reform, as energy audits are currently not followed up by the preparation and implementation of measurable energy-saving action plans by the audited firms. Finally, the Czech government could develop a more systemic approach to green skills development and provide SMEs with stronger guidance in compliance with new sustainability reporting requirements.

1 The business environment

Czechia's economy relies heavily on SMEs, which provide two-thirds of business sector employment. However, they remain significantly less productive than large firms, operating at only about 60% of their productivity levels. In recent years, the Czech government has made progress in reducing administrative burdens, particularly through the digitalisation of company formation, permitting, and licensing procedures. However, further improvements are possible by streamlining current insolvency procedures, strengthening the digitalisation of government services (e.g., through the "once only principle" and a unified digital business ID) and a quicker implementation of digital government portals whose creation has already been planned. Czechia is also modernising its Regulatory Impact Assessment (RIA) system by clarifying methodologies, but the system would benefit from a more consistent application, enhanced public consultation, and ex-post evaluation. Finally, broadening the simplified tax regime beyond self-employed individuals to include smaller SMEs could ease compliance and support the transition to an employer status.

Key messages

- **SMEs account for a large share of the Czech economy but are less productive than large firms**. SMEs account for two thirds of business sector employment, but the average SME is only 60% as productive as the average large firm.
- **Czechia's administrative burden has decreased in the past years, but the pace of improvement could further accelerate.** Administrative processes related to company formation, as well as permitting and licensing, have been streamlined and digitalised. Between 2018 and 2023, Czechia improved by six places in the administrative burden indicator of the OECD Product Market Regulation (PMR) index, reaching the sixth place among OECD countries. Nevertheless, there is still room for improvements. Some of the business life events, such as those surrounding insolvency, have received less attention and could be further streamlined and digitalised.
- **Czechia could also accelerate the digitalisation of government services.** A top priority should be ensuring that Czechia has the adequate digital infrastructure in place to respect the "once-only principle" (i.e., asking companies for the same information only once), and that this be linked to a digital business ID. Czechia's ratings of digital government infrastructure have not improved much in recent years. Several critical digital infrastructure portals (e.g., the Entrepreneur's Portal and the Single Control Record Portal) are at various stages of development and should be completed as soon as possible, with a view to further streamlining the business environment for local companies.
- **Czechia's Regulatory Impact Assessment (RIA) approach could be further strengthened.** Czech authorities are currently working on streamlining the RIA methodology and making it easier to understand and follow. Such efforts are worthy and should continue. Authorities could consider three other measures to improve the process: applying RIAs more often and more consistently, improving public consultation (for instance, by building an online consultation portal), and applying ex-post assessments more consistently.
- **Finally, Czechia could consider broadening its simplified tax regime to a wider segment of the SME population.** The country has a simplified tax regime for self-employed individuals (i.e., people running a business without employees). Creating a simplified regime for smaller SMEs could smoothen the transition from self-employed to employer SMEs and decrease the compliance costs associated with taxation. Depending on the design, such a scheme might have a small budgetary impact, as only 10% of national firms pay the corporate income tax.

Business environment conditions

SMEs account for two-thirds of business employment, but are less productive than large firms

Like in other EU countries, SMEs account for a large part of the national economy in Czechia, but they are less productive than large firms. SMEs account for the vast majority of firms (99.9%) and two-thirds of employment, similar to Poland but more than in Germany. At the same time, the average SME productivity is only 60% as much as that of large firms. Czechia's productivity gap by firm size is larger than Germany's, where SME productivity is two-thirds that of large firms, but smaller than in other Central and Eastern European (CEE) countries, such as Hungary (57%), Poland (51%) and Slovakia (48%). The difference between the productivity of SMEs and large firms was constant in Czechia between 2017 and 2020, whereas it decreased slightly in the other CEE countries (Figure 1.1).

Figure 1.1. SME contribution to the Czech economy

Percentage values

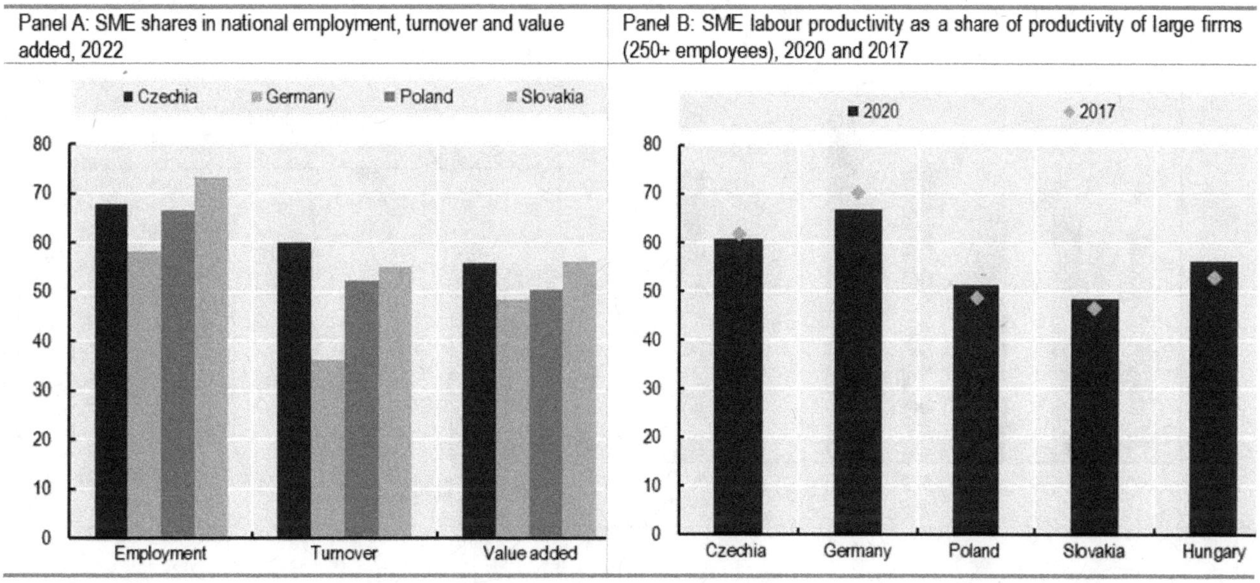

Note: Value added at factor costs refers to 2020 for Czechia and Slovakia and 2021 for Germany and Poland. Numbers refer to the business economy except financial and insurance activities (BTNXK in ISIC rev. 4).
Source: OECD Structural Business Statistics Database

Czechia's business environment improved between 2018 and 2023

A supportive business environment is crucial to closing the productivity gap between SMEs and larger companies. SMEs can be disproportionately affected by regulatory and administrative burdens, as they have fewer resources to spend on compliance. Reducing these barriers, alongside improvements in access to finance, access to skills and digitalisation, can free resources for SMEs to invest in improvements in efficiency and innovation, boosting productivity and growth.

Czechia's business environment improved between 2018 and 2023, as measured by the OECD Product Market Regulation (PMR) indicator (Figure 1.2, Panel A). The indicator, which contains a variety of measures, including the administrative and regulatory burden and the governance of state-owned enterprises, improved slightly in absolute terms and maintained Czechia's position in the top third of OECD member countries. The most marked improvement was in the simplification of the administrative and regulatory burden, where Czechia leapt from the 24th place in 2018 to 9th place in 2023 among OECD member countries (Figure 1.2, Panel B).

Figure 1.2. The OECD Product Market Regulation (PMR) indicator, Czechia and selected countries, 2023 and 2018.

Absolute values of the PMR indicator (Panel A) and Czechia's ranking compared to other countries (Panel B)

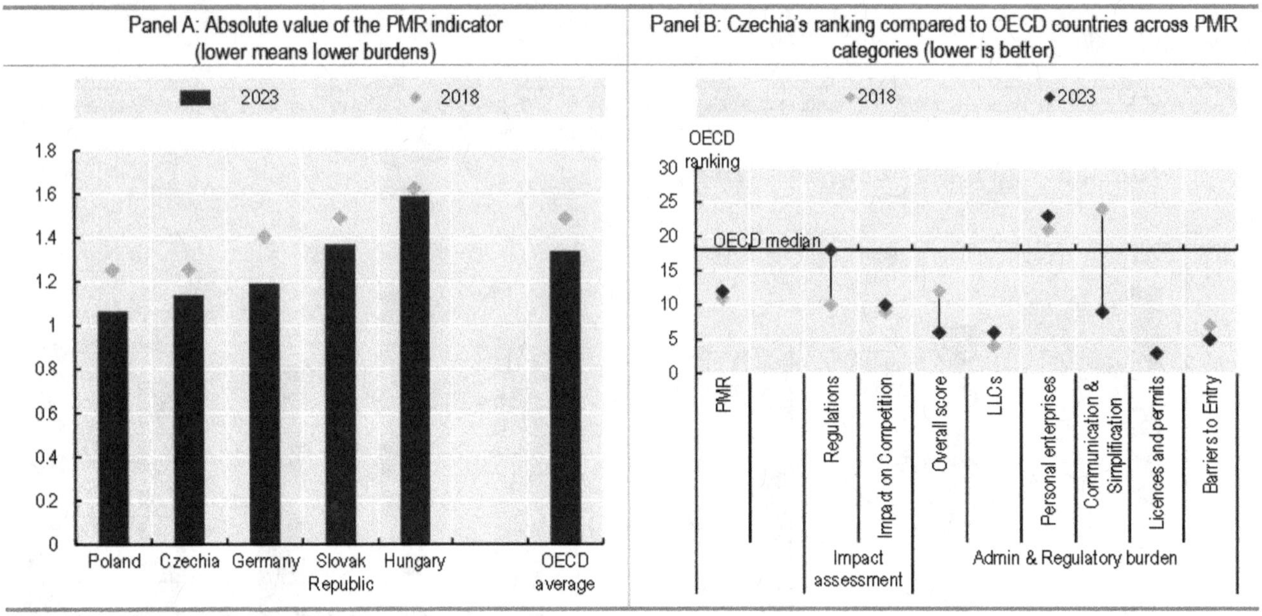

Note: LLC stands for limited liability company. The LLC and personal enterprises scores refer to the administrative and regulatory burden of setting up such companies.
Source: OECD Product Market Regulation Database

Complexity and the uncertainty surrounding policy decisions remain important challenges

The complexity and uncertainty of administrative and regulatory requirements remain important issues for Czech businesses. According to a 2024 Eurobarometer survey, 72% of Czech firms identified the complexity of administrative procedures as a barrier to doing business in the country, above the EU average (66%) and higher than in Poland, Germany and Hungary. Similarly, 60% of Czech firms cited fast-changing legislation and policies as problems when doing business in the country, slightly below the EU average of 64% (see Figure 1.3, Panel A).[1]

Figure 1.3. Administrative complexity and uncertainty in Czechia and selected countries

Panel A: The share of businesses reporting the indicator as a problem, 2024	Panel B: Czechia's eGovernment indicator ranking compared to EU average

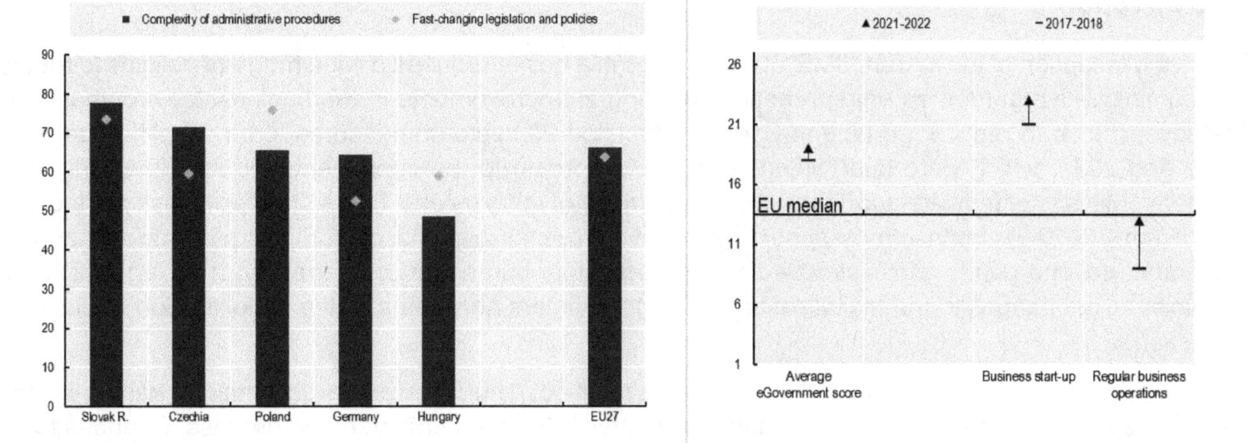

Note: Both indicators are based on survey evidence. For Panel B, lower scores are better.
Source: Eurobarometer (European Commission, 2024[1]) for Panel A and eGovernment indicators (European Commission, 2023[2]) for Panel B.

High uncertainty regarding government policy typically deters investments and can discourage compliance. Compliance with policies and regulations is costly and increases the cost of doing business. In cases of regulatory uncertainty, firms might decide to risk not complying at all with rules and regulations. One example of policy causing uncertainty was the repeal of the obligation to submit the VAT control statement (*Kontrolní hlášení DPH*) in 2023. The obligation, which had been imposed in 2016, required firms to declare detailed transactional data to the tax authorities. To do so, firms had to invest in technical infrastructure such as electronic invoicing systems. Despite this initial investment, representatives of the business community viewed the system positively, as it levelled the playing field by limiting the scope for tax evasion.[2] However, the government repealed this policy in 2023, citing too many administrative burdens and a decrease in cash transactions. The sudden reversal clearly penalised the firms that had invested in the electronic invoicing system and recreated more room for tax evasion.

Czechia needs to accelerate the digitalisation of its government services

The pace of digitalisation in government services could accelerate. E-government services are a crucial instrument for cutting red tape and ensuring a hassle-free business environment. However, Czech businesses did not have, as of 2024, access to a one-stop shop that would allow them to manage their most common life events, such as start-up, licenses, taxation and hiring. According to the European Commission's eGovernment benchmarking indicators, Czechia's ranking in e-government services saw a decline relative to other European countries between 2017 and 2022, to the 23rd position in the EU, despite improvements in absolute values (Figure 1.3, Panel B). Despite a similar improvement in e-government services for regular business operations, the country's ranking dropped even further, from the 9th position to the 13th position in the EU.

Czechia has reduced the administrative burden for firms and should continue efforts in this direction

Since the inception of the current SME Strategy, Czechia has introduced a wide range of policies to reduce the administrative burden on entrepreneurs, resulting in improvements in the business environment. For instance, a plan to reduce red tape in Czechia identified 90 sectoral measures to be simplified between 2019 and 2021, which were later widened to 124 according to the implementation reports of the SME Strategy (Ministry of Industry and Trade, 2019[3]; Ministry of Industry and Trade, 2022[4]; Ministry of Industry and Trade, 2023[5]). Such efforts should continue across all aspects of administrative reform and be expanded beyond purely administrative costs to regulatory burdens more generally, from legislative and administrative changes to the digitalisation of the government services and the simplification of business processes.[3]

The steps to set up a company have also been simplified. The requirement to obtain a trading license before registering a company has been abolished, shortening the duration of the process. Changes to the Notary Code have made it possible to establish a company entirely online without having to meet a notary in person.[4] The government has made available examples of articles of association, further decreasing the information costs for setting up a company. In addition, changes to the beneficial ownership regulation[5] have made it possible to register beneficial owners free of charge and make subsequent changes online in simple cases.[6]

Nonetheless, the process of setting up a business could be further simplified. First, entrepreneurs could benefit from a portal where they could submit all registration online. While there is a website which informs potential entrepreneurs of the process for starting a business (www.businessinfo.cz), there is no such portal to upload all documents for central processing. Registering a business still requires a notary's approval, which can be done online but slows down the process and increases costs. Other countries, such as Denmark and Estonia, have completely digitalised and automated the process of setting up a company, with no need for the presence of a notary.[7] Second, VAT registration should be accelerated and simplified. It is currently a separate process that can take up to a week, and stakeholders met during the project mentioned that this has not improved much in the past years.

The licensing process has also been simplified through the elimination of some requirements considered superfluous. Examples include the health card for employees in food-related activities and the requirement for employees in non-risk professions to undergo regular occupational medical examinations, which were both abolished in 2023.[8] Furthermore, a digital Trade Licensing Portal was launched, where businesses can find all the information and forms related to trade licensing. The Trade Licensing Portal is linked to the Citizen's Portal, so people can, in principle, also obtain their license online.

A new Building Law, which came fully into force in July 2024, should simplify the process of obtaining a construction or building permit. The new law allows the permitting process to be completely digitalised and combines previous separate processes, such as zoning and building, into one streamlined procedure. An online one-stop shop for building permits called the Builder's Portal (https://portal.stavebnisprava.gov.cz/) aims to bring together the builders and the authorities, digitalising the entire process and connecting separate databases such as the land register and the water register.[9]

Other events in a company's life have received less attention from policymakers and could further improve. Czechia's insolvency framework could still improve the treatment of entrepreneurs who have failed once, as well as the prevention and streamlining of the bankruptcy process (André and Demmou, 2022[6]).[10] In 2019, the average insolvency procedure took more than two years, in line with the European Union average (European Commission, 2019[7]). Similarly, the process of liquidations could be further streamlined, to improve the recovery of assets. Between 2015 and 2018, the recovery procedure took one year longer than the EU average, which was three years (European Banking Authority, 2020[8]). The net recovery rate of SME loans in insolvency procedures was also low, standing at 12% or almost a third of the weighted EU average (33%). Liquidating a company takes at least four months even for small companies, as the law stipulates a waiting period of 90 days once the intention of liquidation is made in the Commercial Bulletin, to allow creditors to come forward and make their claims.[11] Streamlining the insolvency and liquidation processes could provide more certainty to both creditors and entrepreneurs, as well as ensure that business closing does not prevent entrepreneurs from starting new businesses.

Czechia could accelerate the digitalisation of government services

The level of government digitalisation is in line with the EU average and there are several large projects in development which should further improve this dimension. Several large public digitalisation projects are being developed as part of the Recovery and Resilience Plan (RRP), and these should provide more efficient government services and improve the business environment for firms once they are completed (Box 1.1). The European Commission's eGovernment Benchmark[12] for regular business operations placed Czechia at 80%, in line with the EU average and with virtually no improvement between 2018-2019 and 2021-2022. The development of digital platforms such as the Entrepreneur's Portal and the Information Obligations Database is expected to improve the e-government services for businesses, but this should become visible in future iterations of the benchmark indicator.

Box 1.1. Digital portals currently under development by the Czech government

The Entrepreneur's Portal, which was in Phase 1 (documentation and design) as of 2024, should further simplify the process of setting up and managing a business and act as a one-stop shop for entrepreneurs. The government is developing the portal internally, by partnering with the Czech Digital and Information Agency (DIA) and the National Agency for Communication and Information Technologies (NAKIT).

The partnership provides several advantages. First, it should speed up development, as the government can bypass the need to organise complex tenders which could take a long time. As of 2024, the plan was expected to be operational in Q2 2026. Second, the partnership benefits from the Agency's experience in developing the Citizen Portal (*Portál občana*), the digital one-stop-shop for citizens. The Agency intends to re-use some of the work from that project, promoting an efficient use of resources. Third, the partnership ensures that public authorities continue to develop digital capabilities internally. Fourth, it should ease the connection between the entrepreneurship portal and other digital portals, either existing or in development, such as the Single Control Record Portal.

The Single Control Record Portal, which was also in Phase 1 as of end 2024, should allow public authorities to co-ordinate their inspections. The aim is to limit disruptions to businesses and allow communication between public authorities and businesses. The Record is also scheduled to be operational in the first half of 2026. As of 2024, the supplier had won the technical tender and Phase 2 (development) was scheduled to start at the beginning of 2025.

The Information Obligations Database (IOD) should provide businesses with an overview of legal obligations in a user-friendly language. The portal, which should provide links and explanations regarding general business requirements, is scheduled to be available to the public in 2025 and was in the final testing phases as of the second half 2024.

Some of the digital portals have developed more slowly than initially expected. Some solutions such as the Single Control Record Portal, which aims to co-ordinate firm inspections across government bodies, require complex inter-institutional communication, and the required legal clarifications have taken longer than expected.

Other portals have stricter deadlines, due to their funding structure. The Single Control Record Portal and the Information Obligations Database (IOD) are funded through the Recovery and Resilience Plan (RRP), so they have strict deadlines and requirements for development, which will need to be met as part of the funding agreement.

Czechia could investigate the feasibility of further improvements in the digital government infrastructure, such as a unique electronic ID (eID). An electronic ID recognised by all government entities should further simplify the processes of starting, managing and closing a business. Using a digital ID across all government services would limit the need for notaries in the process of setting up a business and allow seamless integration of other business services, such as licenses and permits and business de-registration. Furthermore, it could easily connect the information in the business registry, tax offices and employment offices with information from the upcoming portals (e.g. Single Control Record Portal, Entrepreneur's Portal), allowing the creation of an ecosystem of digital government solutions accessible through a single digital ID.

Czechia should improve the Regulatory Impact Assessment (RIA) methodology, as well as the consultation and ex-post assessment processes

Czechia has a well-developed methodology for Regulatory Impact Assessment (RIA) and could consider adopting it more systematically. Czechia's overall RIA score, based on the OECD "Government at a Glance" indicators, has been stable around 2.7 out of 4 for the past decade, placing the country in the top quarter among OECD countries and above the OECD average (Figure 1.4, Panel B). Czechia scores especially well on the oversight and transparency of RIA (7th place in the OECD in 2021, see Panel A relative to other countries). However, it only ranks in the 22nd place with respect to the RIA methodology and its systematic adoption. In fact, full RIAs are only required for draft laws proposed by the government and those expected to have significant impacts, as decided by the RIA Board of the Government Legislative Council (OECD, 2021[9]). Other draft laws and regulations, such as those proposed by Members of the Parliament or subnational authorities, do not need to be accompanied by full RIAs.

Figure 1.4. The Regulatory Impact Assessment (RIA) process in Czechia and selected countries, 2021 and 2017

Panel A: Indicators of Regulatory Policy and Governance (iREG) Absolute values, 2021	Panel B: Czechia's iREG indicators relative to other OECD countries (lower is better)

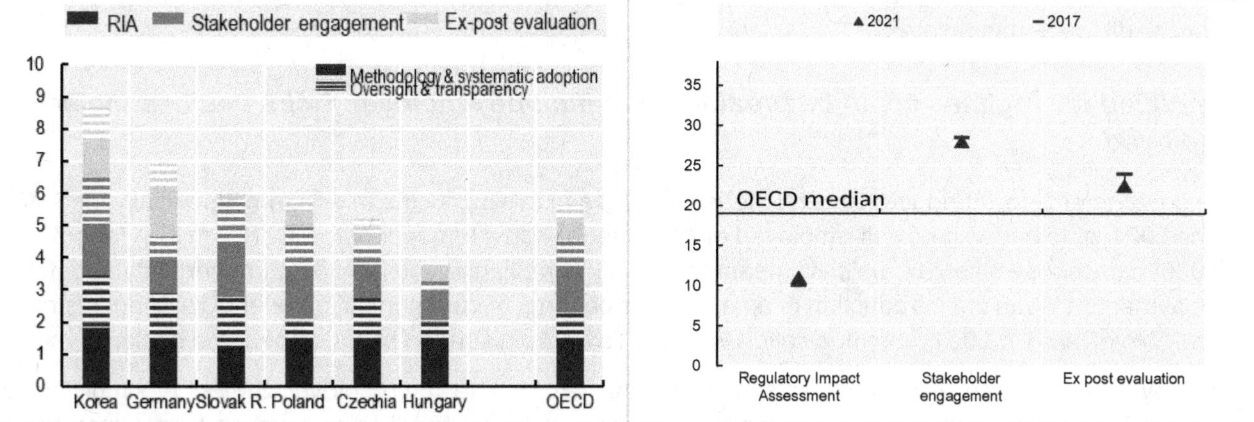

Note: For each category of regulatory tool (RIA, stakeholder engagement, ex-post evaluation), two composite indicators were taken into account, which can run from a minimum of 0 to a maximum of 2: (i) methodology and systematic adoption, represented in solid colours. Methodology scores how close is the existing methodology of the category to the best practices. Systematic adoption records the formal requirements for regulatory tools such as RIA or stakeholder engagement to be conducted, and how often that happens and (ii) oversight and transparency, represented in a striped pattern. Oversight records mechanisms to monitor and ensure the quality of the tool, while transparency covers the openness of the process. The total value for a tool is given by the sum of the two indicators, i.e. the sum of the striped and solid bars of the same colour.

Source: Source: OECD Government at a Glance Indicators 2023 (OECD, 2023[10]).

Czechia's stakeholder engagement in the lawmaking process could also be improved. In 2021, the country ranked 28th among OECD countries for stakeholder engagement (Figure 1.4, Panel B). Both sub-indicators of the quality of stakeholder engagement (methodology and systematic adoption; oversight and transparency) score in the bottom third across OECD countries (28th place). The consultation process is not standardised, nor is it compulsory for all pieces of legislation. Consultations are part of the RIA process, so they are mandatory for laws initiated by the executive branch and those expected to have significant effects. For laws initiated by other bodies, such as the Parliament or subnational authorities, RIAs are not mandatory, which also makes public consultations not mandatory. Finally, there is no online portal for stakeholders to provide feedback, which can discourage participation by the civil society, including business associations and single entrepreneurs.

Ex-post evaluation of policies and laws could also improve. Czechia ranks 23rd among OECD countries on ex-post evaluation and close to 20th in the OECD for both subcomponents of the index (Figure 1.4). It is not clear to what extent the results of RIA assessments are reflected in the final result of the legislative process, as the RIA Board does not receive feedback on how the RIA reports have been used. The provision of such feedback could encourage a stricter adherence to better regulation guidelines along the entire policymaking process.

As of mid-2024, the government was evaluating and revising its RIA methodology; however, it is unlikely that the revisions will address all the abovementioned issues. Authorities expect the new methodology to streamline the RIA process and ease compliance with improved regulatory guidelines.[13] However, there is no expectation that the RIA consultation process will change, nor are there any clear plans to build a public consultation portal or to standardise the consultation process. Similarly, there are no plans to communicate how the results of the consultation process feed back into the lawmaking process, and it is unclear whether the ex-post evaluation will be systematically applied to inform future legislative proposals.

A digital portal for public consultations could improve many of the issues affecting the current consultation process. It would facilitate stakeholder feedback on legislative proposals, thereby fostering their engagement. It would also increase transparency, showing both the stakeholder feedback and the responses of policymakers, thus allowing stakeholders to view different drafts and how they reflect past feedback[14]. Importantly, a digital portal could also help standardise the consultation process, providing clear deadlines and templates.[15]

Simplified tax regimes could be broadened to include employer SMEs besides the self-employed

The government has introduced several measures that aim to simplify the tax system, especially for SMEs. Since 2021, sole traders and self-employed entrepreneurs with a turnover below CZK 2 million (about EUR 80 000) can choose a flat tax, which is meant to simplify compliance and provide more certainty about their tax payments.[16] With the introduction of an electronic channel of communication on the Tax Administration portal (*MojeDane*) in 2021, communication with the Tax Administration has also become easier.

The government could also consider simplifying the tax regime for employer SMEs. A simplified (or presumptive) regime could decrease compliance costs for SMEs while limiting revenue losses, provided it is carefully designed (Mas-Montserrat et al., 2023[11]). Three issues stand out regarding simplified tax regimes for SMEs: the scope, the conditions, and the transition out of the simplified regime into the standard one.

Regarding the scope of the simplified tax regime for SMEs, the threshold for qualifying should be low enough to target SMEs, but broad enough to avoid adding too much complexity in definitions. Some presumptive tax regimes for SMEs define a list of excluded activities, typically sectors with average high revenue and sufficient ability to pay and comply, such as financial and real estate services or liberal professions. Eligibility criteria should also include provisions against business splitting, thus preventing the use of the simplified regime for tax avoidance. For example, in turnover-based tax regimes, firms may have an incentive to split before reaching the turnover threshold to maintain eligibility. To avoid such issues, countries typically include provisions limiting the number of businesses that a single taxpayer can manage under a simplified regime or define eligibility criteria to include all the business income of a taxpayer across all their owned or managed businesses. Argentina's *Monotax* regime allows qualifying taxpayers to manage maximum three business units. Another alternative to limiting business splitting can be found in Colombia's *Simple,* which applies the income eligibility threshold to all the businesses managed or owned by an applicant to the simplified tax regime and excludes companies that have split in the last five years (Mas-Montserrat, Colin and Brys, 2024[12]).[17]

There are also multiple options for the conditions of the simplified tax regime, which are usually based on turnover thresholds. The simplest is a *lump-sum regime*, which requires (very small) firms to pay a fixed amount of tax. While such systems provide a simple way of calculating tax liabilities for small firms, they pose a disproportionate burden on firms with low or negative profits and can worsen the cash position of firms, especially during downturns. A *flat tax regime* requires a proportion of a pre-defined tax base, usually a share of the turnover, and is the more preferred option in the case of high-income countries. Flat tax regimes are expected to better reflect the ability of businesses to pay taxes but require businesses to introduce some minimum accounting standards and greater oversight by tax authorities. If eligibility is based on turnover and the threshold is high, progressivity should be considered, for instance through pre-defined brackets. Since simplified regimes typically limit the possibility of deducting business expenses from the tax liability, some sectoral differentiation might also be warranted to account for differences in profitability across sectors (Mas-Montserrat, Colin and Brys, 2024[12]). For instance, Poland's flat-rate tax regime (*Ryczałt*) varies based on the source of income – from 17% of turnover for the income of freelance professionals to 2% for revenue derived from agricultural activities.

Another alternative is to calculate the tax payment based on a range of *activity indicators*. These systems require more administrative capacity but can, in theory, better approximate a firm's ability to pay taxes. They are, however, more complex, as they require measuring multiple indicators and ensuring their accuracy. For instance, Spain's simplified system (*Módulos*) calculates the due tax payment by using several indicators linked to the business activity (e.g. turnover, number of employees, surface area, kilometers traveled, etc.).

Finally, best practices suggest that simplified regimes should provide a smooth transition to the standard tax system, for instance through grandfathering clauses[18] or some transition period between the two regimes. A gradual transition can avoid sudden changes in tax complexity and tax burdens for firms when crossing the threshold of the simplified regime, thus easing the transition to the standard tax system (Mas-Montserrat, Colin and Brys, 2024[12]).

Brownfield development for business real estates should receive more attention

Brownfield regeneration has been a government priority for the past two decades. The first National Strategy for Brownfields Regeneration was adopted in 2008, with the current version covering the period 2019-2024.[19] The Business and Investment Development Agency, CzechInvest, has developed a useful tool for potential investors, in the form of a public database of brownfield sites. The website www.brownfieldy.cz offers an overview of mapped brownfield sites, with details such as surface area, photos, and ownership type (public or private). At the beginning of 2025, the database included 4 458 brownfield sites, with an average size of three hectares.

The main focus of Czechia's brownfield strategy has been to access and implement EU projects rather than develop brownfields more generally (Ministry of Industry and Trade et al., 2019[13]). This focus has remained in the period 2019-2024, although brownfield development has lost importance in the list of government priorities. As of mid-2024, most government-financed projects related to brownfield development referred to lands under public administration, which are only 20% of all brownfields, as opposed to private brownfields, which account for 60% of the total. The Ministry of Regional Development has developed some calls for brownfield development by municipalities and towns, but they have mostly covered the development of brownfields for non-business use.

The development of private brownfields has also been slow. Since 2021, the government has set up the Brownfield Fund, a publicly support venture capital fund providing financing to brownfield revitalisation projects that aim to construct business premises in the Moravian-Silesian region. In total, the National Recovery Plan allocated CZK 500 million for brownfield sites for business use, but only CZK 110 million had been used by the end of 2022 and seven projects had received funding by 2023.

Accelerating the development of brownfields could provide firms, especially SMEs, with more space to develop and grow. While the new Building Law should facilitate the construction permitting process, authorities could consider policies to make the private development of brownfields more attractive. Such policies could go beyond development subsidies and include regulatory fast-tracks for the building process and dedicated support for co-ordinating all stakeholders involved in the land management process, from municipalities to landowners. Alternatively, Czech authorities could consider a brownfield development task force, which could provide other public authorities with the information required for developing brownfields.

Box 1.2. National business environment reforms from an EU legislation perspective

Czechia has, in recent years, transposed into national law a range of European legislation that aimed to simplify administrative procedures for SMEs.

With respect to the business environment, Czechia's SME Strategy is broadly in line with the broader European SME Strategy (European Commission, 2020[14]). Both strategies recognise the importance of administrative and regulatory barriers and how they can fall disproportionately on SMEs. However, while the European SME Strategy explicitly articulates the importance of the "Think Small First", "once only" and "digital by default" principles in creating a business environment conducive for SME development, the Czech SME Strategy leaves these principles more implicit. Future versions of the Czech SME Strategy could make the importance of these principles more explicit, encouraging future regulations to be simple, digital, and SME-friendly by default.

Czechia's commitment to regulatory streamlining could also be improved to be more in line with other European strategies, especially when it comes to Regulatory Impact Assessments. For instance, the Communication on long-term competitiveness specifically mentions streamlining EU legislation and regularly assessing it to limit unnecessary burdens (European Commission, 2023[15]). Czechia's future SME strategy could include such a commitment to regularly review and simplify regulations.

Czechia has also transposed a range of Directives into national law. One first example is the Directive 2019/1023 on preventive restructuring, which became effective in September 2023. Preventive restructuring is a procedure which aims to avoid insolvency and enable a company in financial distress to survive by renegotiating new terms with its creditors. With the passing of the new law, companies in Czechia will now be able to use preventive restructuring to avoid formal bankruptcy. Another example is the Digitalisation Directive 219/1151, which was transposed into national law in January 2021. The legislation encourages countries to facilitate the full digitalisation of key events in the life of a company, including by making templates for such events freely available on registration portals. However, the implementation of such portals has been slow, and a digital one-stop-shop for businesses has yet to be fully operational in Czechia.

Conclusion and recommendations

Czechia has significantly improved its business environment over the last decade but could accelerate its transformation to improve SME competitiveness. It should continue the process of administrative and regulatory simplification by streamlining rules and communicating changes in a clear language to firms. It should focus on the development of a digital ecosystem of government solutions, to make its administrative processes more efficient and provide firms with more transparency and certainty regarding standard events in a firm's life (i.e., creation, licensing, development, hiring, bankruptcy, etc.).

Based on the analysis of this chapter, the following policy recommendations are proposed to strengthen the business environment for SMEs in Czechia.

- Accelerate the process of government digitalisation through the development of digital portals for businesses, prioritising the Entrepreneur's Portal and linking it with other business services through the system of the national digital business ID.
- Continue the process of administrative simplification by ensuring regular reviews of existing regulations and processes.

- Apply Regulatory Impact Assessments more often and more consistently by broadening the existing RIA methodology to include consultation and ex-post analysis, creating a public consultation portal, and ensuring that RIA outcomes better inform the policymaking process.
- Further simplify business taxation for SMEs, for instance by introducing simplified requirements and regimes for other SMEs than the self-employed
- Provide regulatory certainty by announcing legislative changes in advance and limiting sudden changes in direction (i.e., forward planning).
- Consider introducing more often private brownfields in national brownfield regeneration programmes through the offer of regulatory fast-tracking, grants or fiscal incentives.

References

Altaxo (2024), *Company Liquidation in the Czech Republic*, https://www.altaxo.cz/en/company-liquidation-czech-republic. [17]

André, C. and L. Demmou (2022), "Enhancing insolvency frameworks to support economic renewal", *OECD Economics Department Working Papers*, No. 1738, OECD Publishing, Paris, https://doi.org/10.1787/8ef45b50-en. [6]

Czech-lawyers.com (2024), *Company Liquidation in the Czech Republic*, https://czech-lawyers.com/company-liquidation-in-the-czech-republic/#:~:text=It%20takes%20approximately%204%20months,liquidation%20in%20the%20Czech%20Republic. [16]

DoMyTax.com (2024), *The liquidation of a company/sole proprietorship in the Czech Republic*, https://firma.domytax.cz/en/changing-ownership-or-liquidation-of-a-company-sole-proprietorship-in-czechia. [18]

European Banking Authority (2020), *Report on the Benchmarking of National Loan Enforcement Frameworks*, https://www.eba.europa.eu/sites/default/files/document_library/About%20Us/Missions%20and%20tasks/Call%20for%20Advice/2020/Report%20on%20the%20benchmarking%20of%20national%20loan%20enforcement%20frameworks/962022/Report%20on%20the%20benchmarking%20of%20nat. [8]

European Commission (2024), *Flash Eurobarometer 543. Business' Attitudes towards Corruption in the EU*, https://europa.eu/eurobarometer/surveys/detail/3180. [1]

European Commission (2023), *eGovernment Benchmark 2023*, https://digital-strategy.ec.europa.eu/en/library/egovernment-benchmark-2023. [2]

European Commission (2023), *eGovernment Benchmark Method Paper 2020-2023*, https://digital-strategy.ec.europa.eu/en/library/egovernment-benchmark-2023. [19]

European Commission (2023), *Long-term competitiveness of the EU: looking beyond 2030.* [15]

European Commission (2020), *An SME Strategy for a sustainable and digital Europe*, https://eur-lex.europa.eu/legal-content/EN/TXT/HTML/?uri=CELEX:52020DC0103. [14]

European Commission (2019), *SBA Fact Sheet Czechia*, https://www.google.com/search?q=SBA+Fact+Sheet+Czechia+2019&rlz=1C1GCEA_enFR1075FR1075&oq=SBA+Fact+Sheet+Czechia+2019&gs_lcrp=EgZjaHJvbWUyBggAEEUYOTIHCAEQIRigATIHCAIQIRigATIHCAMQIRigATIGCAQQIRgVMgcIBRAhGI8CMgcIBhAhGI8CMgcIBxAhGI8C0gEIMTUwNmowajeoAgCwAgA&s. [7]

Mas-Montserrat, M., C. Colin and B. Brys (2024), "The design of presumptive tax regimes in selected countries", *OECD Taxation Working Papers*, No. 69, OECD Publishing, Paris, https://doi.org/10.1787/58b6103c-en. [12]

Mas-Montserrat, M. et al. (2023), "The design of presumptive tax regimes", *OECD Taxation Working Papers*, No. 59, OECD Publishing, Paris, https://doi.org/10.1787/141239bb-en. [11]

Ministry of Industry and Trade (2023), *Annual Report on the Implementation of the SME Support Strategy in the Czech Republic 2022*. [5]

Ministry of Industry and Trade (2022), *Annual Report on the Implementation of the SME Support Strategy in the Czech Republic 2021*. [4]

Ministry of Industry and Trade (2019), *Plan for Systemic Reduction of Administrative Burden on Business for the Period 2019 - 2022*, https://www.mpo.gov.cz/assets/cz/podnikani/regulace-podnikani-a-snizovani-administrativni-zateze/2019/7/Plan-snizeni-AZP-do-roku-2022.pdf. [3]

Ministry of Industry and Trade et al. (2019), *National Brownfield Regeneration Strategy*. [13]

OECD (2023), *Government at a Glance 2023*, OECD Publishing, Paris, https://doi.org/10.1787/3d5c5d31-en. [10]

OECD (2021), *OECD Regulatory Policy Outlook 2021*, OECD Publishing, Paris, https://doi.org/10.1787/38b0fdb1-en. [9]

Notes

[1] The share of firms that find the complexity of administrative procedures a problem is 66% in Poland, 64% in Germany and 49% in Hungary. For the uncertainty of rules and policies, the numbers are 76%, 53% and 59%, respectively (European Commission, 2024[1]).

[2] These insights were obtained during the OECD fact-finding mission, which took place in June 2024. Roundtable participants also mentioned that the costs for installing the e-invoicing infrastructure were between EUR 3 000 and EUR 6 000, a significant amount, especially for smaller SMEs.

[3] Broadening the programme to reduce administrative burdens to other regulatory costs was also mentioned in the 2021 Regulatory Policy Outlook (OECD, 2021[9]).

[4] See Act 300/2021, amending Act 358/1992 amending 358/1992 and recent amendments to Act 634/2004.

[5] The beneficial owner is the person who ultimately owns a company, either directly or indirectly. According to European legislation (Directive 2015/849), a shareholding of more than 25%+1 share or more than 25% in the customer held by a corporate entity counts as being a beneficial owner.

[6] In simple cases, the registration of the beneficial owner takes place automatically from the commercial register, so there is no need for the entrepreneur to take further steps for the registration.

[7] However, it can also be argued that the presence of a notary in the process of business creation can also offer advantages, for instance providing advice on the articles of association or provisions for conflict resolution.

[8] Further information available at: https://dostupnyadvokat.cz/en/blog/what-expect-from#povinnost.

[9] A similar streamlining related to environmental permits for construction should further simplify the administration for construction processes.

[10] In 2023, Czechia introduced a new legislation on preventative restructuring, which implemented Directive EU 1023/2019 on preventative restructuring frameworks. This should improve the indicators regarding the prevention and streamlining of bankruptcy, but as of early 2025, the most recent data was from 2022.

[11] Accounting and law firms start the pricing of a basic voluntary liquidation at CZK 35 000, with the price increasing with the complexity of the case. Some firms quote a starting price of EUR 1 500 or CZK 35 000 (Czech-lawyers.com, 2024[16]; Altaxo, 2024[17]) but other websites geared towards foreign clients quote EUR 2 500 (DoMyTax.com, 2024[18]).

[12] The eGovernment benchmark score is the average across four key dimensions (user centricity, transparency, key enablers, cross-border services), which is mostly obtained through mystery shopping and using the actual online government services. Some of those key dimensions are calculated as the average of further indicators. For instance, user centricity is the weighted average between online availability (67%) and user support (33%), each consisting of two sub-sub-indicators. Sub-indicators are determined by benchmarking against a best-practice scenario, which has a maximum score of 100% (European Commission, 2023[19]).

[13] There are also plans to develop a curriculum for public servants to learn how to apply the new methodology, but this has been delayed, first by the pandemic and then by shifting priorities.

[14] Needless to say, lawmakers are not obliged to take on board all stakeholders' feedback, but it is generally good practice to report which feedback was positively received and which one was not, possibly offering a reason for it.

[15] Past OECD reports have already suggested standardising the consultation process and stimulating stakeholders to participate in consultations (OECD, 2021[9]).

[16] The choice between a flat tax and a lump-sum tax is permanent, i.e. taxpayers cannot easily choose to switch between the two depending on their yearly income.

[17] To avoid issues associated with business splitting, most simplified tax regimes that apply to incorporated businesses only apply to companies held by natural persons (Mas-Montserrat, Colin and Brys, 2024[12]).

[18] A grandfathering clause is a provision which allows old rules to apply for a finite time to existing or past situations, while the new rules apply to the new situations. Such clauses are typically used to smoothen the transition towards the new rules, as the new regime gradually becomes the dominant one.

[19] The current National Strategy for Brownfields Regeneration can be found on CzechInvest's website (in Czech): https://www.brownfieldy.cz/app/uploads/2023/08/nsrb-2019-2024-20190708.pdf

2 SME financing

Czechia performs below the EU average when it comes to SME access to bank loans, credit guarantees and equity finance. Credit market conditions worsened in 2023-24 due to surging interest rates meant to tackle higher inflation. Demand for credit guarantees is high among Czech SMEs, yet delivery is constrained by resource limitations within the national development bank, which also manages priority programmes for the green and digital transition of the business sector. Equity gaps are particularly acute at the early stage, where venture capital and angel investment remain limited. New venture capital policies, notably through a fund-of-funds approach, have aimed to expand early-stage finance for start-ups, as have recent regulatory improvements on crowdfunding, corporate bonds and the junior stock market. Additional measures, such as tax incentives for equity investors and the development of hybrid financing instruments, would further support these efforts. State-owned institutions providing trade finance offer valuable support but are constrained by stringent regulation. Finally, a more consistent combination of financial instruments with advisory services in government programmes would enhance SME capabilities and improve the effectiveness of public support.

Key messages

- Like in other EU countries, higher interest rates following the 2022-2023 energy crisis have negatively impacted the cost of business lending for SMEs in Czechia, resulting in reduced investment activities and a shift towards internal financing. **Access to external finance remains challenging, with the country ranking below the EU average in terms of SME access to loans, credit guarantees, and equity.**
- **There is a significant gap in the offer of equity finance for SMEs, particularly in early-stage ventures**. Venture capital and business angel investment volumes are low in Czechia, thus limiting the growth potential of innovative SMEs. Additional support measures, such as targeted tax incentives for early-stage investors, could stimulate the development of the equity market, at a limited cost to the government.
- **Several regulatory measures have been implemented to improve access to finance**, including new regulations for crowdfunding, corporate bonds, and Employee Stock Ownership Plans (ESOPs). However, more can be done to expand the capital market and provide better support for early-stage investments.
- **The demand for credit guarantees among SMEs is high, but the current supply is hindered by financial and staff constraints in the national development bank**, which is in charge with the implementation of the main current credit guarantee schemes, as well as with other priority programmes targeting the green and digital transition. Although green and digital programmes for SMEs are current priorities, it would be important not to overlook a widely used programme like the national loan guarantee scheme, which could be expanded so as to have a limited fiscal impact.
- **VC policies in the form of funds-of-funds have been introduced by the Czech government to support innovative start-ups. However, the capital market remains underdeveloped, so additional measures, such as tax incentives for equity investors, would be recommended**. Expanding the activities of the National Development Bank (NRB), including the development of hybrid financial instruments, could also enhance the access by entrepreneurs to early-stage financing options.
- **The START platform for SME listings works well, but additional support services could enhance its effectiveness**, in particular through a network of dedicated advisors to guide SMEs in their listing process. In this regard, the Initial Public Offering (IPO) fund is a positive initiative that aims to stimulate SME access to equity financing through public matching of private investments in the junior stock exchange.
- **State-owned institutions like the Czech Export Bank (ČEB) and the Export Guarantee and Insurance Corporation (EGAP) play a small but useful role in providing trade finance to SMEs**. Their operations are currently limited by a restrictive regulatory framework, which could be adjusted to offer greater flexibility and support for internationally oriented companies. However, this different role will require a change in the oversight entity of these institutions, currently the central bank, which needs to follow EU capital-market stability rules for all its supervised institutions.
- **While financial support is crucial, complementing it with non-financial measures such as mentoring, advice, and counselling can significantly enhance its effectiveness**. Providing SMEs with the necessary knowledge and skills to navigate complex financial landscapes is often essential for business growth and would align Czechia with international good practices.

SME financing conditions

SME credit conditions are tight

Like other EU countries, Czechia has been characterised in recent years by higher inflation and higher interest rates, which have had a negative impact on the cost of business lending for SMEs. Based on information from the latest edition of the OECD SME and Entrepreneurship Financing Scoreboard, there is evidence that Czech companies have reduced investments and/or have used internal sources of finance to carry out investments (OECD, 2024[1]). The Survey on the Access to Finance (SAFE) of the European Central Bank (ECB) supports this argument, with most enterprises reporting tightening credit conditions, as well as rising input costs and shortages in skilled labour (European Central Bank, 2024[2]).

According to the European Investment Fund (EIF), Czechia ranks relatively low in the main SME financing indicators (Figure 2.1). The EIF SME Access to Finance (ESAF) Index, which monitors the state of SME financing markets in the EU, has consistently placed Czechia in the lower tier among EU countries, reflecting longstanding challenges that Czech SMEs face in accessing external finance, such as high interest rates for small loans (i.e., below EUR 250 000) and a large proportion of SMEs reporting barriers in access to finance (Torfs, 2023[3])

Figure 2.1. The EIF's SME access to finance index across EU countries, 2022

Composite indexes

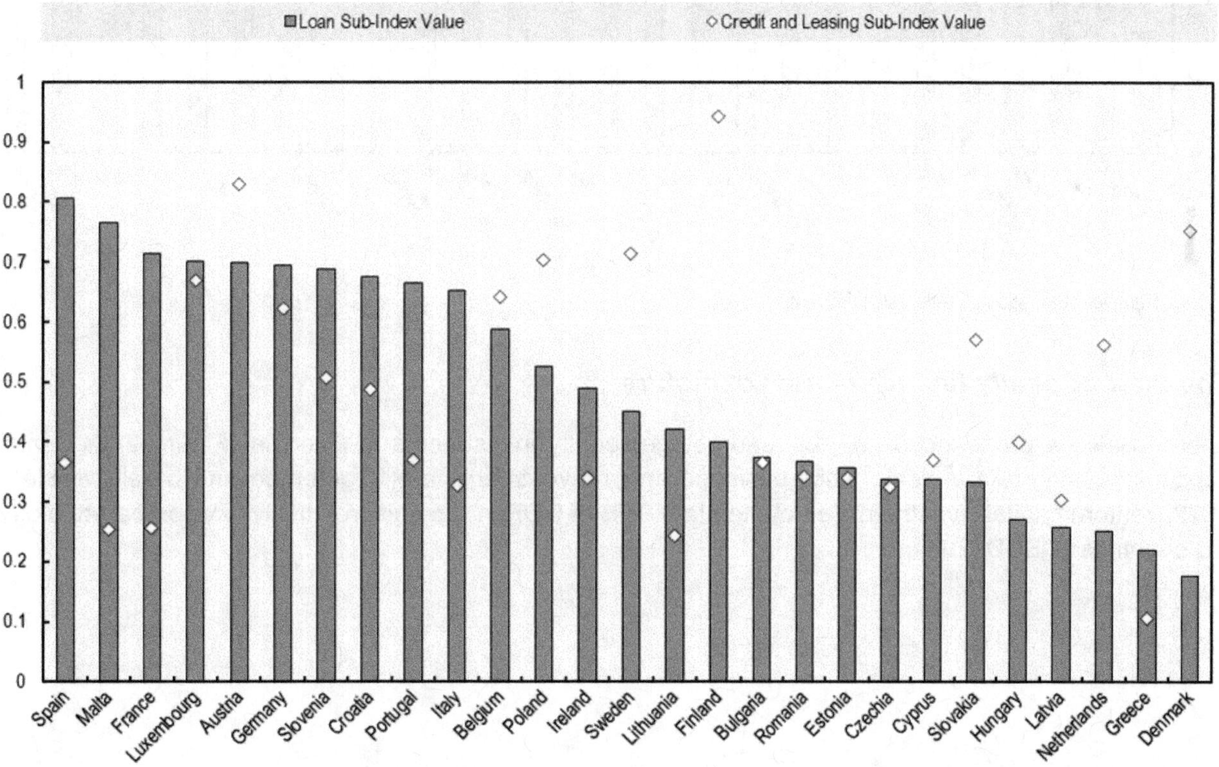

Note: The EIF SME Access to Finance Index (ESAF) is a composite index that aggregates multiple indicators related to SME financing. A higher value (closer to 1) implies more favourable conditions for SME financing, while a lower value (closer to 0) suggests greater challenges in accessing finance.
Source: OECD based on (Torfs, 2023[3])

It follows that private-sector credit is relatively modest compared to other high-income countries (Figure 2.2). While these data can be interpreted in several ways, they may point to restricted access to finance for non-financial corporations, which could be the result of strict lending standards, high interest rates, or a small appetite for small business lending among financial institutions.

Figure 2.2. Credit to non-financial corporations at market value, 2023

Percentage of GDP

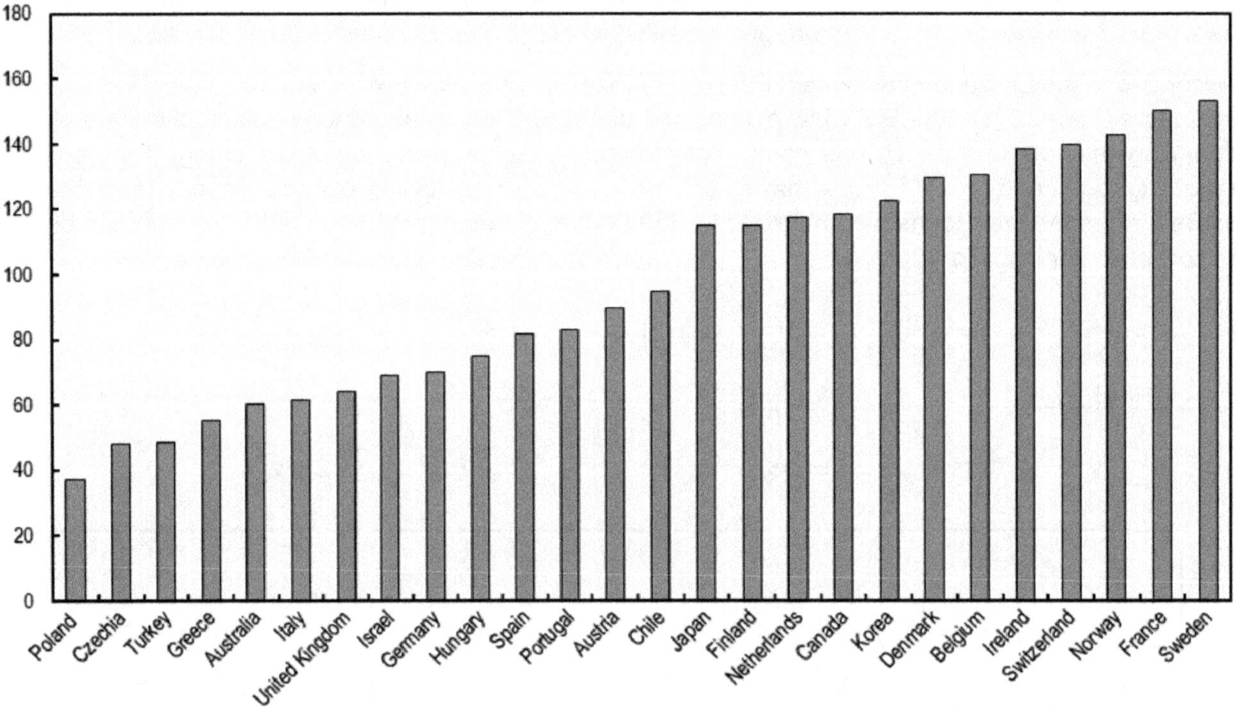

Source: Bank for International Settlements (BIS) data

The offer of equity finance is not yet mature

There is also a pronounced gap for (early-stage) equity investments in Czechia (Figure 2.3). Venture capital investments are weak, while business angel investments are fragmented and barely visible. In 2022, venture capital investments amounted to 0.04% of GDP in Czechia, relatively low compared to other EU countries (OECD, 2024[1]).

Figure 2.3. Business angel investment and VC investments across EU countries, 2022

A: Business angel investments per inhabitant, 2022 | B: Venture capital investments as a percentage of GDP, 2022

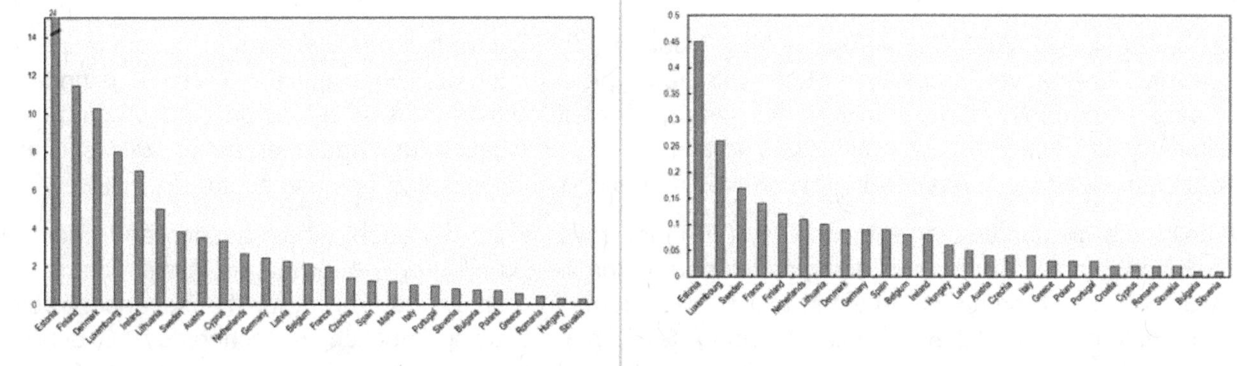

Notes: Population data are sourced from Eurostat

Source: https://www.eban.org/eban-annual-statistics-compendium-for-2022/; https://www.eif.org/news_centre/publications/eif_working_paper_2023_92.pdf

SME financing policies: Mid-term evaluation of the national SME Strategy

The government has made significant progress in the implementation of the national Capital Market Action Plan

The "National Strategy for the Development of Capital Market in the Czech Republic, 2019-2023" has made a number of recommendations to stimulate the nascent national capital market in Czechia (Czech Ministry of Finance, 2019). Some recommendations have led to concrete actions and changes to the regulatory framework that are relevant to high-potential SMEs in need of capital market financing.

First, the government has implemented Regulation 2020/1503 on European business crowdfunding, and the central bank (Czech National Bank, CNB) has granted the operating license to four entities. The Regulation has had the merit of bringing clarity about the rules applicable to crowdfunding platforms, including consumer protection[1].

Second, a new regulation has been enacted for corporate bonds whose value is below EUR 1 million (sometimes referred to as "mini bonds") that do not require a prospectus. The regulation now mandates that these bonds must also have an International Securities Identification Number (ISIN) to enhance transparency. The issuance of an ISIN requires the company to obtain a Legal Entity Identifier (LEI), which is linked to anti-money laundering (AML) procedures.

Third, the National Strategy also seeks to address the education of retail investors about capital markets. The government approved the National Strategy for Financial Education 2.0 in January 2020, which had previously been prepared by the Ministry of Finance. While this new Strategy covers a broad range of target groups and topics, the role of the capital market and long-term investments for households with savings are both covered, as was suggested in the National Strategy for the Development of the Capital Market.[2]

Fourth, another recommendation in this Strategy was to create an association of Czech business angels, which was established in 2019 (the Czech Business Angel Association), not long after the publication of the National Strategy.

Fifth, the law has also been amended to introduce Employee Stock Ownership Plans (ESOPs) (January 2024). ESOPs provide employees with an ownership interest in the company through the offer of company stocks typically available at preferential price. Besides non-financial benefits, such as increasing employee retention, ESOPs offer SMEs a financing mechanism that can help raise capital without relying only on external investors or creditors.

Sixth, Act No 462/2023 Coll., effective from 1 January 2024, introduced a new form of pension fund, the so-called Alternative Participation Fund. This new type of fund has fewer regulatory restrictions (in terms of assets and fees) to invest in asset classes such as infrastructure, real estate and, above all, private equity funds.[3] Although, as of mid-2025, no alternative participation fund had been set up, this legislation sets the conditions for channelling more investments into domestic start-ups and scale-ups.

Finally, the distributed ledger technology (DLT) initiative, which will enable the issuance and trading of SME bonds across Europe, is being developed under the EU pilot regime for market infrastructure. This regulation, which came into effect in March 2023, aims to create a framework for the issuance, trading, and settlement of digital assets, including SME bonds, using blockchain technology. Czechia is participating in this initiative by aligning its regulatory framework with the EU's pilot regime. In fact, the Czech Central Securities Depository Prague was the first institution in the world to be allowed to operate the DLT Settlement System under the DLT Pilot Regulation. This means that entities operating in the Czech capital market can apply for authorisation to operate DLT-based platforms, facilitating the issuance and trading of SME bonds. This could enable Czech SMEs to access new forms of financing through tokenised bonds, potentially increasing their funding options and liquidity.

The role of credit guarantees could be strengthened

Czechia's credit guarantee scheme has been effective but could be further expanded to satisfy unmet demand. The National Development Bank (*Národní Rozvojová Banka*, NRB), which is the public development bank of Czechia, offers various tailored guarantee schemes to support SMEs:

- *Inostart*: This guarantee is designed for innovative startups (less than three years old) seeking loans of up to CZK 15 million, with guarantees covering up to 80% of the loan.
- *M-záruka*: This guarantee is available for established SMEs needing financial support for investment or operational projects. It covers up to 70% of the loan amount, capped at CZK 5 million.
- *Záruka* ZRS (Development Cooperation Guarantee): This guarantee is aimed at businesses expansion into developing markets outside the EU. This scheme supports projects in infrastructure and agriculture, covering up to 50% of the loan, depending on the project's risks.
- Electromobility Guarantee: It supports businesses investing in electric vehicles or infrastructure like charging stations to promote sustainable practices (see also the chapter of the report on the green transition of SMEs).
- Smart Guarantees for Digitalisation: It helps SMEs modernise their operations through digital transformation projects, offering guarantees for technology and software-related loans.
- *Záruka* ZRS (for Social Enterprises): It is tailored for social enterprises focusing on social impact initiatives, including employment and social inclusion projects.
- The Flood Guarantee: It offers SMEs a guarantee for an investment or operating loan to help with the restoration of business after floods.
- The *Vadium* Guarantee: It reduces the amount of funds that SMEs must deposit as security when bidding for a public contract.

These schemes are provided free of charge for eligible businesses. Demand for these products is significantly higher than the available supply, and Czechia's volume of credit guarantees, in relative terms, is below the volumes observed in other countries (0.19% of GDP in 2021). In addition, the current guarantee streams are meant for specific purposes, which means that many SMEs in need of credit to meet working capital requirements or more general investment needs are not eligible to apply.

Figure 2.4. Credit guarantee volumes in selected countries, 2021

Percentage of GDP

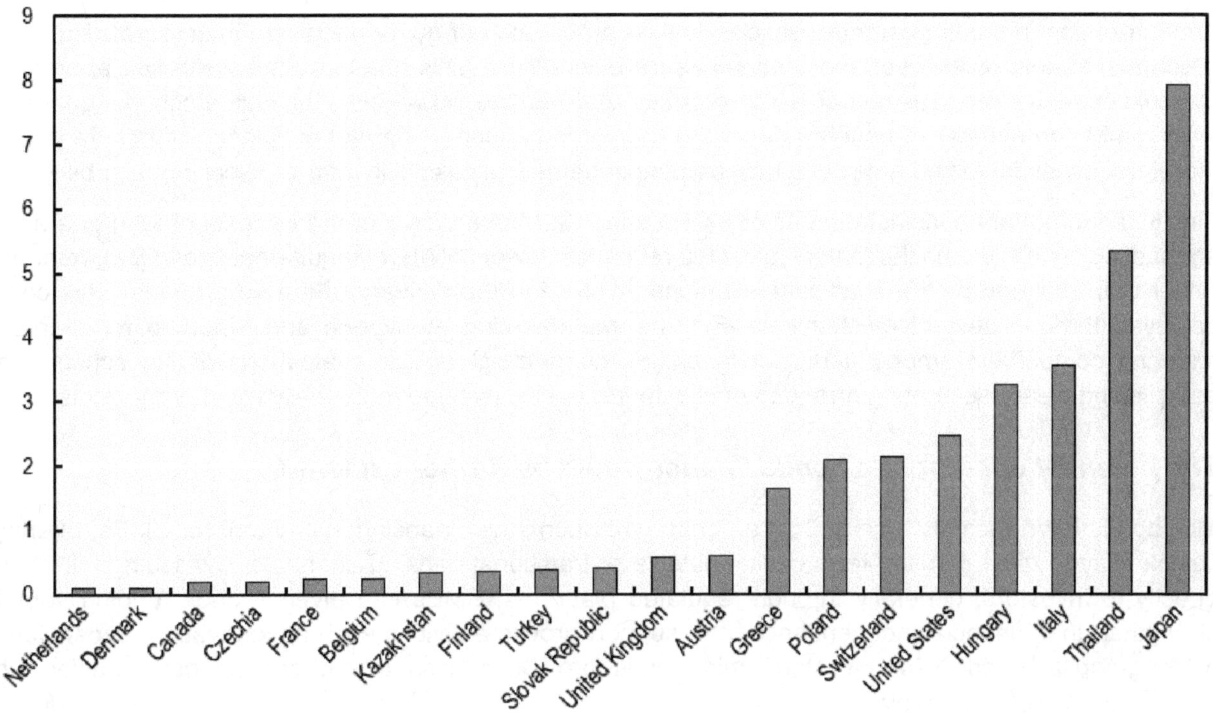

Source: (OECD, 2024[1])

A 2024 survey from the national Association of Small and Medium-Sized Enterprises and Crafts (AMSP ČR) confirms that 40% of Czech companies in need of credit find it difficult to obtain such credit without a state guarantee. Interestingly, the percentage is the highest among mid-sized companies (50-249 employees), manufacturing firms, and businesses that have benefited from guarantees in previous years.[4] This last point suggests that some companies may have become dependent on government-backed guarantees for their operations.

Under the previous programming period, the Czech government was operating a more extensive credit guarantee scheme through the *Expanze* Guarantee Fund, which was positively regarded by representatives of the Czech business community interviewed for the preparation of this report. The volume of this fund was EUR 336 million and was matched by a loan fund with the same name totalling EUR 426 million.[5] The Czech government should consider re-introducing national guarantee schemes at a similar scale of the *Expanze* Fund. Given the low level of defaults on guaranteed loans, this change would not involve high costs for the government budget. Guarantee schemes do not incur significant costs unless loan defaults are common, which is not the case in Czechia, making them a fiscally efficient form of support compared to direct subsidies.

In the context of Czechia, guarantees are provided free of charge. However, the pricing of credit guarantees often includes application fees and annual management fees, which can be charged to borrowers and/or lenders. The introduction of a more competitive fee structure for the Czech scheme could enhance its cost-effectiveness, allowing the government to offset part of the administrative costs while still providing affordable financing options to SMEs.

While it is possible that some SMEs, particularly the smaller ones, might be discouraged by such fees, this concern can be mitigated through careful design. For example, application fees could be applied only to approved loan guarantees, or deferred until a recipient business has demonstrated a certain degree of stability. This approach would ensure financial sustainability without restricting access, ultimately enhancing the reach and impact of the programme.

Another option in credit guarantee policies is the combination of guarantees with interest rate subsidies, which makes this policy even more attractive for businesses. This has been the prevailing approach in Czechia under the previous guarantee programme. A downside, however, is the higher cost per guarantee, which limits the number of beneficiaries if the budget is capped. A careful evaluation of this trade-off is, therefore, essential to find a balance between the scheme's accessibility and its fiscal sustainability.

Finally, an important consideration involves ensuring that the majority of the benefits of loan guarantees are passed on to SMEs in the form of lower interest rates, lower collateral requirements and longer tenures, rather than retained by the financial institutions involved in the delivery of the programme. This can be achieved through several mechanisms such as implementing monitoring and reporting requirements, fostering competition among participating banks, conducting regular evaluations of the scheme, and establishing clear risk-sharing arrangements with the banks involved in the delivery of programme.

The potential of corporate bonds finance could be further explored

Mini bonds have recently emerged as an important alternative financing instrument for SMEs, offering a flexible way to raise medium-term capital outside of traditional banking channels. By issuing mini-bonds directly to investors, generally through regulated platforms, SMEs can diversify their funding sources, strengthen their financial independence, and support growth activities such as innovation, expansion, or working-capital needs. For investors, mini-bonds provide access to higher-yield opportunities while supporting the real economy.

Although between 2013 and 2023 a total of CZK 634 billion of corporate bonds were issued in Czechia (data from the forensic agency "Surveilligence"), national stakeholders have highlighted that this product is not subject to the same level of protection as other retail investment products, potentially leading to pyramid schemes, frauds or misrepresentation of information.

There are, nonetheless., ways to address these issues. On the demand side, possible measures include requiring bond issuers to meet certain revenue, capital, or profitability levels, or to have a proven business and credit history. On the supply side, corporate bonds, especially mini bonds, could only be made available to qualified investors, based on wealth, income or financial knowledge.

Support measures for early-stage equity investments need scaling-up

The Operational Programme Enterprise and Innovation for Competitiveness (OP EIC), managed by the Ministry of Industry and Trade (MIT), was the predecessor of the Operational Programme Technology and Applications for Competitiveness (OP TAC). As part of the OP EIC Venture Capital Programme, the MIT, in collaboration with the European Investment Fund (EIF), had introduced the OP PIK Fund of Funds to support innovative start-up companies through seed and early-stage finance. The initiative received EUR 40 million from the EIF, which were eventually invested through two newly established VC funds – Nation 1 Fund and Lighthouse Ventures – whose investment period was extended until the end of 2023. Besides securing equity finance, selected start-ups also received advisory and mentoring services, including through an acceleration programme specifically tailored to early-stage projects.[6]

More recently, the Czech government and the EIF launched a new EUR 55 million fund-of-funds initiative financed through the Recovery and Resilience Facility (RRF). The RRFCZ Fund-of-fund is expected to invest in three VC funds following specialised strategies:

- Pre-seed co-investment fund: It will support early-stage start-ups.
- Fintech fund: It will focus on distributed ledger technologies (DLT) applications.
- Technology transfer fund: It will commercialise research from leading Czech universities in artificial intelligence (AI).

These initiatives have strengthened the equity finance landscape in Czechia, making the supply of VC in the Czech market closer to that of other similar-sized EU economies. Following the creation of these funds, VC and growth capital investments peaked in 2021, reaching EUR 751 million, before falling in 2022 (OECD, 2024[1]). The most recent implementation plan of the national SME Strategy notes the ambition to establish two additional funds, which appears to be a reasonable choice to keep momentum behind the growth of the domestic VC market.

The current government initiatives to stimulate the supply of venture capital could be complemented by targeted tax incentives for early-stage equity investors, which would be in line with the Europe Startup Nations Standards Declaration adopted by EU Member States in 2021. Finland and Sweden, for example, have successfully introduced tax incentives that encourage investments in start-ups and SMEs. In addition, the further use of mezzanine finance, subordinated loans or other hybrid instruments could also further support diversification in SME financing sources. International evidence indicates that such instruments, which mix characteristics of debt and equity products, offer unique benefits, especially towards growth-oriented ventures (Thompson, Boschmans and Pissareva, 2018[4]). Despite specific reference to quasi-equity instruments in the national SME Strategy and the annual implementation reports of the Strategy, these instruments are not currently used in Czechia.

Finally, the Czech Government could follow the lead of countries such as Denmark and Finland to actively involve pension funds in venture capital investments. With the introduction of the Alternative Participation Fund (under Act No 462/2023 Coll.), which allows the participation of mutual pension savings schemes into equity markets, Czechia now has a long-term opportunity to channel more funds into high-growth start-ups.

Some of these options have already been explored in Czechia in the framework of the Startups and Investors Coordination Council established last year by MIT and CzechInvest. In co-operation with the Europe Startup Nations Alliance (ESNA), an analysis of best practices in individual member states was carried out which could offer the basis for the introduction of relevant policy reforms at national level.

The junior stock market "START" works well, but listed companies could benefit from additional support services

Czechia has a dedicated platform for SME listings on the Prague Stock Exchange, which is called START. As typical with such platforms, the START Market provides a simplified regulatory environment and lower listing costs, making it more accessible for SMEs looking to raise funds through public offerings. As of 2024, there were around 15 companies listed on START, a number that has remained relatively stable in recent years.

The National Development Bank (*Národní rozvojová banka*, NRB) has also recently signed an agreement with the Prague Stock Exchange to support SMEs through equity instruments. Specifically, NRB, through its subsidiary National Development Investment (NRI), has established an "IPO fund" to participate in the START market, acting as investor in the Czech stock market between 2021 and 2023. The IPO fund was valued at CZK 330 million (approximately EUR 12.5 million) and was financed by the Operational

Programme Enterprise and Innovation for Competitiveness, managed by the Ministry of Industry and Trade.

Through the IPO Fund, the NRB buys shares issued on the START market by companies that meet its eligibility conditions, for a maximum amount of 30% of the shares bought by private investors. In doing so, the NRB supports the development of the START market and provides high-growth potential SMEs with additional financing through IPOs. Senior representatives of the Prague Stock Exchange have emphasised the importance of this initiative, noting its alignment with the European Commission's priorities for SME equity support.

In terms of business development services, START provides some help, but the approach is not as structured or rigorous as in other countries. The so-called Nomad (Nominated Adviser) system used by the Alternative Investment Market (AIM) in the United Kingdom could be a model to follow. It would encourage more listings and support listed companies through a range of business development services.

Two state-owned organisations provide trade finance products, but their regulatory framework is too binding

The Czech Export Bank (*Česká Exportní Banka,* CEB) and the Export Guarantee and Insurance Corporation (*Exportní Garanční a Pojišťovací Společnost,* EGAP) are two state-owned institutions supporting export activities through specialised trade finance products. Both are supervised by the national central bank, which means they need to comply with EU regulations on the banking sector, including minimum capital requirements (e.g., the Capital Requirements Directive, CRD)[7].

The current regulatory framework limits the activities of CEB and EGAB. As of 2024, the former had roughly ten clients and an outstanding portfolio of about EUR 20 million, while the latter had around 20-30 clients and EUR 10–20 million in outstanding exposure. Both institutions operate at market rates and deliberately maintain small portfolios to reach exporters insufficiently served by private providers while avoiding excessive risk. This approach helps ensure that they complement rather than crowd out private finance, which is appropriate given their limited national funding.

At the same time, while the current regulatory and supervisory framework ensures high standards of financial solidity, it restricts the activities of both institutions more than is typical for an Export Credit Agency (ECA) (Schlögl, Pfaffenbichler and Raza, 2024[5]). An expansion of the mandates of CEB and EGAP beyond traditional export finance – for example, to offer broader support to export-oriented firms – could help address these constraints.

International experience illustrates this. Atradius Dutch State Business operates under a more flexible regulatory framework, which enable it to provide a wider suite of instruments, including credit insurance, re-insurance and financial guarantees[8]. As implied earlier, this higher flexibility and shift in operations will require an important change in the legal nature of these institutions, notably a change in the role of the oversight institution.

Czechia should couple more regularly business advisory services with SME financing support

Financial aid through grants and loans are rarely matched by comprehensive business development services like mentoring or technical assistance in Czechia. OP TAC has included some elements of advisory services, particularly in innovation and technology adoption, but these services are often project-specific and not consistent across all financial support schemes. Other countries and organisations have more consistently combined financial and non-financial support measures, given the existing evidence that this combined approach has stronger impacts on business performance outcomes (see Figure 2.1).

Box 2.1. The case for combining financial and non-financial support: Evidence from Canada

In 2013, Canada's development bank, BDC, sought an independent and measurable evaluation to determine whether its financing and consulting services were genuinely accelerating the success of entrepreneurs. To accomplish this, BDC commissioned Statistics Canada to assess the impact on its clients from 2001 to 2010. Statistics Canada created a longitudinal database comparing BDC clients (the "study group") with non-clients (the "comparison group"). Both groups were matched in terms of factors like age, employment, assets, debt ratio, profit margin, revenues, industry, and geographic location. Statistical regressions were then used to test various hypotheses regarding BDC's influence on business performance, focusing on five key performance indicators: growth in sales, employment, productivity, profits, and survival rates after receiving BDC financing and/or consulting services. The analysis showed that BDC support had a positive impact across all five indicators, with the most significant effect seen when both financing and consulting services were combined. In these cases, BDC clients experienced sales growth that was 8% to 25% higher than that of non-clients.

Source: (Boschmans and Pissareva, 2018[6])

The new regulatory sandbox for fintech companies should be evaluated

In 2024, with support from the National Recovery and Resilience Plan, Czechia launched its first fintech sandbox to provide a controlled environment for legal and technical testing of new fintech solutions. Participants in the sandbox, including SMEs, benefit from a tailored support package that includes regulatory testing plans, legal assessments of their business models, and structured opportunities for dialogue with public institutions and regulatory experts. The sandbox facilitates engagement with the central bank and other authorities to help navigate licensing or compliance issues. Additional support is available in the form of business mentoring, consultancy, workshops, and networking opportunities, including connections to international partners in academia and industry.

The initiative, co-ordinated by CzechInvest, reflects Czechia's recognition that innovative financial products often challenge traditional regulatory frameworks. By supporting early-stage regulatory and technical evaluations, the sandbox helps to reduce time-to-market and improves regulatory certainty for emerging fintech companies.[9]

A 2020 OECD report outlined a comprehensive set of principles that remain highly relevant for guiding the implementation of regulatory sandboxes (Attrey, Lesher and Lomax, 2020[7]). The implementation of the Czech fintech sandbox could eventually be assessed against this set of principles (see Box 2.2).

Box 2.2. OECD principles on regulatory sandboxes

- Set up a cross-sectoral regulatory sandbox: Include activities that fall directly or indirectly under financial authority supervision, without sector-specific restrictions.
- Ensure no regulatory waivers: Apply existing EU and national regulations proportionally without granting waivers or relaxing rules for sandbox participants.
- Establish strong regulatory and supervisory oversight: Ensure operational effectiveness and improve regulatory clarity through the clear appointment of an oversight institution.

- Enable data-sharing capabilities: Develop a regulatory sandbox with potential data-sharing features, subject to the availability of datasets and necessary resources.
- Include a diverse range of participants: Permit licensed companies and those unsure of their regulatory status to test innovative products, with eligibility based on licensing readiness.
- Implement regular consultation during testing: Require ongoing consultations with participants throughout the testing phase to monitor progress and adjust requirements as needed.
- Allow for early termination: Set up provisions for early termination of a project if the risks to consumers or financial stability become too high.
- Develop an exit procedure: Require participants to provide detailed reports upon exit from the sandbox, including the results and potential impact of their innovation.
- Set up a communication strategy: Ensure clear communication to stakeholders regarding the sandbox's purpose, benefits, and operating rules to manage expectations and foster understanding.

Source: (Attrey, Lesher and Lomax, 2020[7])

Box 2.3. SME financing policies from an EU legislation perspective

The European Commission introduced the SME Strategy for a Sustainable and Digital Europe in March 2020.[10] The EC Strategy highlights the importance of diversifying financial instruments available to SMEs, such as loans, guarantees, equity financing, and crowdfunding. It also underscores the role of the InvestEU Programme, which consolidates multiple EU financial instruments, providing guarantees to mobilise private investment. Additionally, the EU SME Strategy promotes initiatives to strengthen SMEs' financial literacy.

The Capital Markets Union (CMU) Action Plan is another crucial piece of legislation at the EU level. It aims to create a more integrated and efficient European capital market, making it easier for SMEs to access equity finance and other non-bank funding sources. The CMU focuses on reducing barriers to cross-border investment, fostering financial integration, and enhancing access to financing for SMEs across Europe. The Action Plan includes some actions that are particularly relevant to SMEs, such as making companies more visible to cross-border investors, supporting access to public markets, and supporting vehicles for long-term investment.

Czechia's SME Support Strategy broadly reflects these EU policy guidelines, especially the priority of diversifying the financing sources available to SMEs, including through capital market initiatives, crowdfunding, and harnessing distributed-ledger technologies. The establishment of the specialised vehicles for SMEs on the Prague stock exchange is also well aligned with the EU priorities in this area.

Nonetheless, there is scope for offering more advisory services, kick-starting the early-stage equity market, and spreading the offer of guarantees. While there has been progress in the support of early-stage equity finance, desk research and meetings with Czech stakeholders suggest that there is still room for further expansion. The InvestEU programme, for instance, supports companies with a higher risk profile that are not well served by commercial lenders. Czechia could participate more actively in this programme, "topping up" the InvestEU Programme with additional national resources and/or designing complementary policies to stimulate early-stage equity financing.

Similarly, the volume of credit guarantees is low in Czechia. At the EU level, these guarantees are provided through various EU programmes, such as COSME (Competitiveness of Enterprises and Small and Medium-sized Enterprises) and the InvestEU Programme, which Czechia could join more proactively.

Third, in line with the recommendations in this report, EU access-to-finance programmes often include advisory services. These services help SMEs improve their financial literacy, investment readiness, and ability to access various funding sources, including EU-backed financial instruments. The InvestEU Programme not only provides financial support but also includes an Advisory Hub offering technical assistance and advisory services, which can serve as a model for Czechia. While some EU-level initiatives like the Enterprise Europe Network (EEN) and the European Innovation Council (EIC) Accelerator offer support to SMEs in Czechia, more can be done to integrate more comprehensively advisory services into the country's SME financing policies.

Conclusions and policy recommendations

Access to finance remains a key challenge for Czech SMEs, especially in terms of equity and quasi-equity funding. While progress has been made through a fund-of-fund approach across the two last EU programming periods, further targeted actions are needed, for example through the offer of targeted tax incentives for investors in early-stage companies.

Recent regulatory changes, such as the introduction of new rules for corporate bonds and crowdfunding platforms, have created a more favourable environment for investment and are aligned with EU policies. Nonetheless, expanding financial and non-financial support services will be crucial for strengthening the financing landscape and promoting sustained business growth and innovation in Czechia.

Against this backdrop, the following recommendations are meant to strengthen SME financing conditions and policies at national level.

- Establish two additional VC funds, as planned in the implementation plan of the national SME Strategy and as recommended by the evaluation of VC support measures funded by OP EIC. Ensure that these funds co-invest alongside private investors and follow international good practices more generally, for example through engagement with the European Investment Fund.
- Offer more advisory support to SMEs seeking listing on the dedicated platform of the Prague Stock Exchange.
- Evaluate the regulatory sandbox for fintech companies against the general principles for regulatory sandboxes set out by the OECD.
- Consider the introduction of a targeted tax incentive for retail early-stage equity investors whose generosity will depend on the specific terms and conditions of the programme (e.g., income tax relief of the investment up to a certain threshold, full or partial exemption from capital gains taxation, etc.).
- Consider the re-introduction of a credit guarantee scheme similar in size to the previous *Expanze* Guarantee Fund. To reach sufficient scale and limit the budgetary impact, the government could consider the application of a management fee for applying companies and reviewing the costs related to the practice of combining guarantees with grant support.
- Investigate the potential to combine financial support measures with business development services to raise the financial literacy and investor readiness of SME beneficiaries.
- Diversify and scale up the activities of the National Development Bank (*Národní rozvojová banka*, NRB), including through the offer hybrid financing instruments.

References

Attrey, A., M. Lesher and C. Lomax (2020), "The role of sandboxes in promoting flexibility and innovation in the digital age", *OECD Going Digital Toolkit Notes*, No. 2, OECD Publishing, Paris, https://doi.org/10.1787/cdf5ed45-en. [7]

Boschmans, K. and L. Pissareva (2018), "Fostering Markets for SME Finance: Matching Business and Investor Needs", No. 6, OECD SME and Entrepreneurship Papers, Paris. [6]

European Central Bank (2024), *Survey on the Access to Finance of Enterprises in the euro area - Second quarter of 2024*, European Central Bank , Franfurt. [2]

OECD (2024), *Financing SMEs and Entrepreneurs 2024: An OECD Scoreboard*, OECD Publishing, Paris. [8]

OECD (2024), *Financing SMEs and Entrepreneurs 2024: An OECD Scoreboard*, OECD Publishing, Paris. [1]

Schlögl, L., D. Pfaffenbichler and W. Raza (2024), *Aligning European export credit agencies with EU policy goals*, European Parliament, Brussels. [5]

Thompson, J., K. Boschmans and L. Pissareva (2018), "Alternative Financing Instruments for SMEs and Entrepreneurs: The case of capital market finance", *OECD SME and Entrepreneurship Papers*, No. 10, OECD Publishing, Paris, https://doi.org/10.1787/dbdda9b6-en. [4]

Torfs, W. (2023), "The 2022 EIF SME Access to Finance Index", No. 2023/92, European Investment Fund, Luxembourg. [3]

Notes

1 See EU regulation on European crowdfunding service providers for business: https://eur-lex.europa.eu/legal-content/EN/TXT/HTML/?uri=CELEX:32020R1503

2 See National Financial Education Strategy 2.0: https://financnigramotnost.mfcr.cz/cs/pro-odborniky/strategicke-dokumenty

3 See text of the law here: https://www.zakonyprolidi.cz/cs/2023-462. For further information, see: https://www.mfcr.cz/cs/financni-trh/bankovnictvi-a-dohled/platebni-sluzby-a-vyporadani-obchodu/aktuality/2023/zverejneni-zakona-kterym-se-meni-zakon-c-256-2004-53518

4 See: https://amsp.cz/107-pruzkum-amsp-cr-40-firem-ma-problem-ziskat-uver-bez-zaruky/

5 Financial Instruments in EU Funds under Shared Management: Czech and Slovak Experience (2024), presentation shared by Czech Authorities. Applications for the Expansion loan programme lasted until mid-

2023.: https://www.dotaceeu.cz/cs/evropske-fondy-v-cr/financni-nastroje/uvery/drive-poskytovane-produkty/program-expanze

[6] Further information at: https://www.dotaceeu.cz/cs/evropske-fondy-v-cr/financni-nastroje/kapitalove-vstupy/fond-fondu-op-pik-(1)

[7] Based on Government Resolution No. 909 (dated 29 November 2023), the government agreed to integrate the National Development Bank (NDB) and the Czech Export Bank (CEB). In the current legal framework, therefore, CEB and NDB are both subject to the supervision of the national central bank.

[8] For further information, see the website and annual report of Atradius Dutch State Business (DSB) https://atradiusdutchstatebusiness.nl/en_NL/knowledge-bank/annual-review/annual-review-2023.

[9] https://practiceguides.chambers.com/practice-guides/fintech-2025/czech-republic. Most of the information is sourced from a PowerPoint presentation which was shared by the Czech Authorities.

[10] See: https://www.europarl.europa.eu/legislative-train/theme-a-europe-fit-for-the-digital-age/file-sme-strategy

3 SME internationalisation

Czechia is a highly export-oriented economy. However, foreign-owned multinational enterprises account for the lion's share of national exports. SME export volumes have also increased over the past decade, but the number of exporting firms has not grown, pointing to the need of enlarging the base of SME exporters. The high share of foreign value added in national exports also indicates that the position of Czech firms in global value chains is predominantly into downstream activities. The overarching objectives of government SME internationalisation policies include enhancing SME internationalisation, promoting higher value-added exports, and supporting more permanent operations abroad. Programme-wise, existing informational and capacity-building tools, such as the Single Digital Gateway, provide valuable information and advisory services for exporters, but their uptake could be increased. Sector-specific training, export alliances and export incubators help pool expertise and transfer export-relevant skills to SMEs. However, some of these measures could be expanded to engage under-represented groups in international trade such as women entrepreneurs. Finally, strengthening FDI-SME linkages in high-growth sectors through supplier development programmes and supply chain finance could accelerate the export competitiveness of Czech SMEs.

Key messages

- **Czechia is an export-oriented economy**, with exports accounting for 72% of GDP in 2023, ranking the country in the 12th position among EU member states. **Exports are dominated by large foreign multinational enterprises (MNEs)**, which generated more than 70% of export volumes in 2022. **The high share of foreign value added in exports indicates that domestic firms are predominantly integrated into downstream segments of global value chains (GVCs),** reflecting Czechia's specialisation in later production stages such as the assembly of intermediate inputs. This is especially true for high-value-added and global sectors, such as automotive and machinery.
- **The SME export performance has improved in volume terms in the last ten years**, with total SME exports increasing by approximately 30% between 2012 and 2022. **However, the number of exporting SMEs has remained constant.** This suggests an increase in average export intensity among existing exporters and their ability to capitalise on favourable global market trends during the 2010s. At the same time, the limited entry of new SME exporters points to the need of strengthening export readiness across a broader segment of the SME population.
- **Czechia's SME Support Strategy is well aligned with the objectives of the National Export Strategy**, which emphasises strengthening SME export capabilities, increasing the share of high value-added exports, and fostering a more sustained presence in foreign markets. **The coherence between the two strategies is reflected in the policy instruments employed**, which aim to develop a supportive domestic and international environment for exporting and to provide SMEs with targeted services and financing solutions to facilitate international expansion.
- **Information-based support tools** (e.g. the Single Digital Gateway, Points of Single Contact, SOLVIT, and the Product Contact Point) **play an essential role in improving SMEs' access to export-relevant information**. **However, utilisation remains limited**, highlighting the need to expand outreach efforts. Implementing and enhancing the "No Wrong Door" principle, as suggested by the National Export Strategy, and disseminating SME export-support services through the networks of business associations could strengthen awareness and uptake.
- **Export incubators and sector-specific export training programmes contribute to building SME capacity for internationalisation, particularly for innovative firms**. These initiatives could be extended to additional sectors and further complemented by **outreach efforts towards underrepresented groups in trade, including women entrepreneurs**, to promote more inclusive participation in international markets.
- **Czech SMEs also benefit from trade missions and economic diplomacy initiatives**. In this respect, an expansion of the geographical coverage of the PROPEA (Projects for the Support of Economic Activities Abroad) programme, which is run by national embassies, would benefit SMEs seeking access to non-traditional or niche markets.
- **Strengthening business linkages between foreign investors and domestic SMEs remains a key priority** for strengthening technology upgrading in local SMEs and increasing the share of Czech value added in national exports. This objective could be achieved by further developing tools such as the supplier database of the national investment agency (CzechInvest) and by re-introducing supplier development programmes, particularly in sectors with strong growth potential, such as electronics and semiconductors.
- **Stronger FDI-SME linkages can also be facilitated through a wider uptake of supply chain finance (SCF) solutions.** This may require regulatory measures to incentivise shorter payment terms of large buyers towards SME clients, as well as technical support, such as SME training on e-invoicing and the development of standardised SCF digital platforms.

SME access to international markets

Czechia is an export-oriented economy, but multinational enterprises take the lion's share of national exports

Czechia's exports of goods and services accounted for 72% of national GDP in 2023, placing Czechia in the 12th position among EU countries in this specific indicator, ahead of Poland (58%), but behind Hungary (81%) and the Slovak Republic (91%) in the region of Central and Eastern Europe (CEE) (Figure 3.1)[1]. Despite a small drop in the share of GDP over the past decade (four percentage points), Czechia remains more reliant on foreign markets than many other EU economies. The most important export destinations of Czech goods and services are primarily within the EU, with Germany accounting for 9.7% and the Slovak Republic for 4.5% of total exports in 2022.[2]

Figure 3.1. Exports of goods and services in Czechia and selected countries, 2023 and 2012

Percentage of GDP

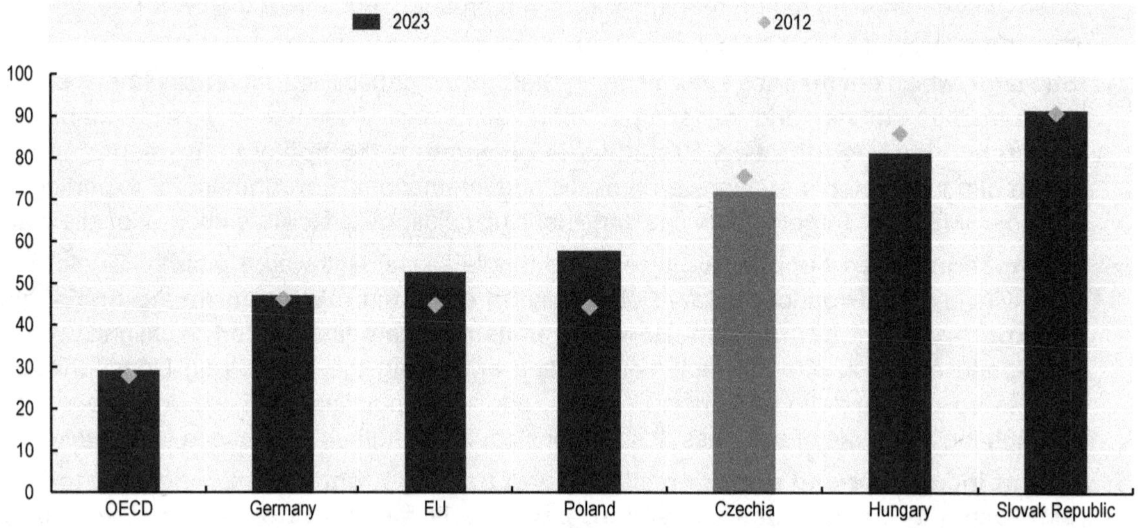

Source: World Bank national accounts data, and OECD national accounts data files, https://data.worldbank.org/indicator/NE.EXP.GNFS.ZS

Large enterprises, particularly multinational enterprises (MNEs), dominate Czechia's export landscape; in 2022, foreign-owned firms accounted for more than 70% of the country's export volume. Foreign-owned firms also derive much larger shares of their sales from exports. The export intensity of foreign-owned firms is nearly double that of domestic firms in the manufacturing sector. This gap remains significant also across other industries such as transportation and storage, information and communication, and construction (OECD, 2024[1]).

A recent OECD analysis of FDI-SME linkages in Czechia shows that the country participates in global value chains predominantly through backward integration, measured by the share of foreign value added in exports, which stands at 39% (OECD, 2024[1]). In contrast, forward integration – measured by the share of Czech value added in other countries' exports – stands at 20%, similar to the OECD average. Higher-than-OECD-average backward participation and relatively lower forward participation suggest that Czech firms occupy a downstream position in global value chains, mostly focusing on using imported intermediate inputs and assembling goods (OECD, 2024[1]).

SME export volumes have increased, but the number of SME exporters has remained stable

Between 2012 and 2022 the overall volume of SME exports increased by around 30% in Czechia, more than Germany (16%), but less than neighbouring economies such as the Slovak Republic (68%) and Poland (75%). Over the same period, the number of exporting SMEs remained quite stable, growing by only 1% (Figure 3.2, Panel B)[3]. As a result, existing SME exporters have expanded their export capacity, but few more companies have started to export.

More generally, SMEs still account for a small share of total exports in Czechia, with micro-enterprises (1-9 employees) contributing approximately 4% and small firms (10-49 employees) 9% of direct exports – both values falling short of the EU averages of roughly 11% for each of the two firm-size categories (Figure 3.2, Panel A). Going forward, it will be crucial to support especially small-sized enterprises to enter foreign markets, as micro-enterprises typically have fewer internationalisation opportunities due to lower average productivity as well as prevalence in non-tradable sectors (e.g., retail trade).

Another issue affecting SME internationalisation in Czechia is the fragmentation of its business sector, which lacks the same numbers of medium-sized enterprises (50-249 employees) as other EU economies (OECD, 2024[1]; OECD, 2021[2]), whereas these companies are the most likely in the SME population to export or to become suppliers of large multinational enterprises, thus adding national value in total exports.

Czech SME internationalisation policies should, therefore, not only target existing small enterprises, but also strive to expand the number of mid-sized companies through appropriate scale-up policies, tackling broader issues such as business-friendly taxation and regulations, access to finance and digitalisation that are discussed in more detail in other chapters of the report. Business scale-up and internationalisation, especially in relatively small open economies like Czechia's, often go in parallel.

Figure 3.2. Share of export volume and number of exporting enterprises by firm size, 2022

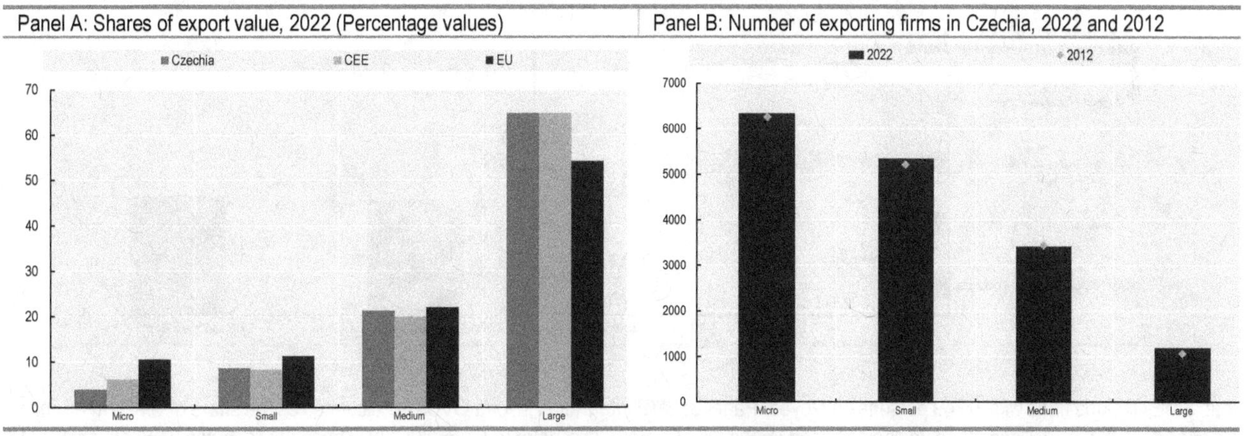

Note: Micro = 0-9 employees, Small =10-49 employees, Medium = 50-249 employees, Large = 250 or more employees
Source: Trade in goods by enterprise characteristics by economic activity and size class, OECD, OECD Data Explorer • Trade in goods by enterprise characteristics by economic activity and size class.

Czech SMEs struggle to enter highly competitive FDI-driven sectors

Most export activity by Czech SME is concentrated in manufacturing, which accounts for 57% of total SME export volumes. Key sub-sectors include the production of fabricated metal products (10% of total SME exports), including machinery and equipment (7% of total SME exports). On the other hand, while automotive is the main exporting industry of Czechia (28% of total exports in 2022), SMEs only contributed

5% of the industry's total exports, pointing to the dominance of large companies in this sector (Figure 3.3, Panel A).

It is generally acknowledged that focusing only on direct exports underestimates the participation of SMEs in international trade, as these companies can also contribute indirectly by supplying MNEs in the context of global supply chains. In addition to avoiding trade-related costs, this indirect participation allows SMEs to benefit from access to cheaper inputs and foreign technologies (López González, 2017[3]). According to available data from 2014, Czech SMEs contributed 47% of the total value added of Czech exports, behind other CEE economies such as Poland (50%), Hungary (52%), and the Slovak Republic (56%) (OECD, 2024[1]).

A recent OECD analysis on FDI-SME linkages in Czechia adds some further nuances, arguing that a major challenge is the limited engagement of Czech SMEs in long global value chains (GVCs) (Figure 3.3, Panel B) (OECD, 2024[1]). Long GVCs integrate various stages of production – e.g., sourcing raw materials, manufacturing components and assembling final products – across wide geographical areas. Participation in long GVCs, therefore, reflects the economy's exposure to highly internationalised sectors (OECD, 2024[1]). Prominent examples include the machinery and automotive sectors, where Czechia-based companies hold a sizeable share of direct exports. However, as described above, large MNE dominate these industries, pointing to an important role for public policies to help Czech SMEs integrate further these supply chains, especially in higher value-added activities such as precision manufacturing, automation integration and quality assurance[4].

Figure 3.3. Top 5 SME manufacturing exporting sectors and SME participation in long GVCs in Czechia, 2022

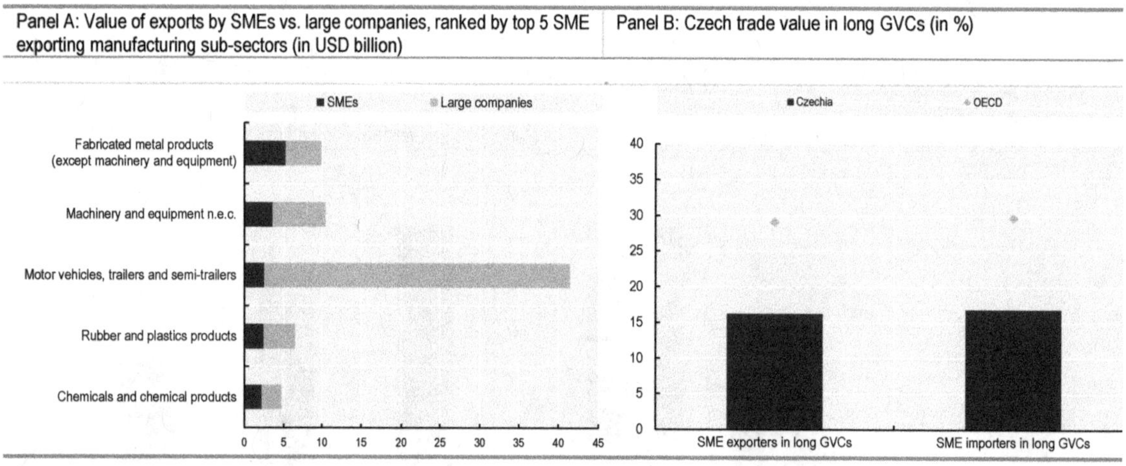

Note: SMEs include firms with 1-249 persons employed. Panel B: SME integration in long GVCs is calculated as the share of SMEs in all imports and exports of the top 10 longest value chains based on the OECD Inter-Country Input-Output (ICIO). These are manufacturing of: textiles (13), wearing appeal (14), leather and related products (15), rubber and plastics products (22), basic metals (24), computers, electronics, and optical equipment (26), electrical equipment (27), other machinery & equipment (28), motor vehicles, trailers and semi-trailers (29), and other transport equipment (30).
Source: Trade by Enterprise Characteristics (TEC) databases, and (OECD, 2024[1]), *Strengthening FDI and SME Linkages in Czechia*, OECD Publishing, Paris, https://doi.org/10.1787/4c97d104-en.

SME internationalisation policies: Mid-term evaluation of the national SME Strategy

The objectives of the new National Export Strategy are closely aligned with those of the SME Support Strategy

The Czech government has recently published a new National Export Strategy ("Export Strategy of the Czech Republic, 2023–2033"), whose objectives appear to be closely in line with those of the National SME Support Strategy, notably those of the chapter on "access to markets". The new Export Strategy shifts from a narrow focus on export promotion to a broader agenda of internationalisation, aiming to help businesses, especially SMEs, establish a lasting and diversified presence in foreign markets through the offer of high-quality final products, services, and integrated solutions. The new National Export Strategy, therefore, prioritises the quality over the quantity of exports and, in doing so, seeks to further the diversification of Czech exports away from an overreliance on EU markets. The Export Strategy also moves from a traditional sector-based approach to a technology-based approach, emphasising cross-cutting technology areas like advanced manufacturing (e.g., 3D printing), artificial intelligence (e.g., autonomous driving), the circular economy, and smart solutions (e.g., smart cities).

The National Export Strategy gathers its specific instruments under two main pillars: a) Developing a pro-export internal ecosystem and improving the external environment; b) Providing services and financing that support firms' expansion abroad.

The first pillar focuses on tailored export support along the business internationalisation journey and applies the "No Wrong Door" principle to ensure that SMEs can access the services they need at different stages of their business lifecycle. This pillar also addresses the external environment by focusing on the improvement of bilateral trade relations. The second pillar covers export-relevant information tools, training, marketing, consulting services, and finance.

Building on these broad areas, the new National Export Strategy identifies specific measures targeting SMEs, many of which are also mentioned in the National SME Support Strategy, suggesting that the two are aligned also with regard to promotional activities and not just objectives. These activities include developing sourcing services for supplier companies, creating tools to support the internationalisation of innovative SMEs and startups, and institutionalising co-operation with the National Development Bank (*Národní Rozvojová Banka*, NRB) to enhance SME support.

The main instruments to support SME internationalisation in Czechia are discussed in greater detail in the rest of this section. The assessment is done against chapter 3 (Access to Markets) of the national SME Support Strategy, whose broad objectives and proposed activities are, as abovementioned, closely aligned with those of the new National Export Strategy of Czechia.

A number of tools provides SMEs with relevant export information, but their outreach could be improved

A range of tools and resources has been developed to help SMEs operate effectively within the EU market and access information on exporting opportunities. Significant progress has been made, for example, on the completion of the Single Digital Gateway. This pan-European electronic signpost gives Czech businesses and citizens access to essential information, administrative procedures, and assistance services needed to operate in other EU countries. For example, SMEs can use the search function on the "Your Europe" portal to obtain tailored information by selecting their target country and topic, such as product requirements, certification, and other rules related to goods. The Single Digital Gateway plays a pivotal role in equipping SMEs with the information necessary to enter EU markets, serving as a critical first step toward successful exporting. SMEs also benefit from the European Commission's

"Access2Markets" portal, which offers comprehensive and up-to-date information on trade conditions with non-EU countries, including tariffs, quotas, rules of origin, and import procedures.

Beyond these two portals, the national government has introduced three support services meant to facilitate the operations of local SMEs in the EU market.

First, the Point of Single Contact (PSC) offers free support to SMEs and individuals by providing key information on service-provider requirements, authorisations, and formalities needed to start and operate a business in the EU. The PSC also gives access to contacts for relevant authorities, guidance on EU-wide service rules, dispute-resolution and consumer-protection information, as well as links to practical assistance such as the European Consumer Centres Network. Accessible online or in person at 15 regional trade licensing offices, the PSC handled around 1 900 inquiries in 2021 and nearly 2 200 in 2022, reflecting growing demand.

Second, SOLVIT is a free, primarily online service run by national authorities across the EU to help individuals and businesses resolve problems caused by public authorities in another member state. It aims to close cases within 10 weeks when they involve a breach of EU rights and have not yet gone to court. SOLVIT handled 183 cases in 2021 and 109 in 2022. While total cases fell due to the pandemic, business-related cases increased.

Third, the Product Contact Point (ProCoP) offers free information on technical requirements for placing products on the EU market, including guidance on the principle of "mutual recognition" and contacts for competent authorities. It supports both foreign firms exporting to Czechia and Czech firms exporting abroad. Although requests were relatively low during the pandemic (194 in 2021 and 114 in 2022), ProCoP remains an important resource for SMEs navigating product regulations and restrictions affecting the free movement of goods and workers.

Overall, these information tools and portals play an important role in making local SMEs aware of rules and regulations involved in entering foreign markets, but there is room for improving their visibility and outreach as the overall number of users remains low compared to the much larger base of potential exporters. This could be achieved by strengthening the "no wrong door" principle which aims to enable SMEs to access all relevant services seamlessly at multiple entry points, as suggested in the National Export Strategy. Furthermore, a comprehensive document could be developed to consolidate SME support tools. This resource would offer clear, detailed information on available tools, training programmes, and export financing options. It could be widely circulated by well-connected partners, including business associations and Chambers of Commerce, to ensure broader outreach and accessibility for SMEs.

Export training by CzechTrade supports the internationalisation efforts of SMEs, increasingly also outside the EU market

CzechTrade is the government trade promotion agency of Czechia and, as a result, plays a central role in supporting the internationalisation of local SMEs. CzechTrade has traditionally focused on the promotion of direct exports, but in recent years its portfolio has expanded to include assistance for establishing a more permanent presence in foreign markets, not only traditional EU markets but also emerging markets.

A key instrument in this expanded support model is the network of export incubators. Since 2021, CzechTrade has progressively opened incubators in strategically selected markets, initially in India, followed by the United States, the United Arab Emirates and Mexico. These incubators offer practical services such as marketing, communications, and operational guidance to help companies enter and adapt to local markets. Typically, each incubator supports 5-10 companies per year, although utilisation levels vary: some, like the one in Chicago, face overcapacity, while others, like Bangalore, experience lower demand.

The selection of the locations of incubators aligns with the new National Export Strategy, which encourages firms to explore a broader range of export destinations beyond traditional markets like the EU. This shift is intended to give SMEs greater flexibility in choosing markets that match their capabilities, including specific strengths in niche technologies, while supporting Czechia's broader objective of export diversification.

Besides the incubator programme, CzechTrade continues to offer a wide range of export-readiness training for SMEs, some of which are sector-specific, such as the Design Centre for companies in the creative industries (Box 3.1), while others cover new thematic areas such as compliance with ESG requirements (see also chapter 7 on the green transition).

Box 3.1. CzechTrade's Design Centre

The Design Centre of CzechTrade facilitates connections between the creative industry and other business sectors by linking companies with professional designers and offering advisory services and guidance. The Centre collaborates closely with the Ministry of Industry and Trade and is a member of the Bureau of European Design Associations (BEDA), which provides Czech companies with access to the latest insights on design theory and practice. The centre specifically supports the competitiveness and internationalisation of firms through national exhibitions, participation in international design fairs, and educational and research activities (e.g., seminars, symposia, and conferences). Event and trainings are offered free-of-charge.

Source: Website of the Design Centre CzechTrade: https://www.czechtrade.cz/sluzby/design-centrum-czechtrade .

Some social groups, like women entrepreneurship, could be the target of specific support

CzechTrade's initiatives to support SME internationalisation could be further strengthened by undertaking targeted actions to support underrepresented groups in trade, particularly women entrepreneurs. Recent OECD work shows that women entrepreneurs in the EU are about 19% less likely than men to have customers in another country (OECD/European Commission, 2023[4]). This points out that trade liberalisation has differentiated impacts due to unequal access to resources and established gender roles in society (European Parliament, 2024[5]). Gender disparities are also evident in other statistics. In 2022, Czechia's national self-employment rate was 15%, but only 11% for women. Furthermore, only 13% of self-employed women had employees, a figure below both the national average (16%) and the much higher EU average (32%) (OECD/European Commission, 2023[4]). These gaps suggest that there is scope for targeted programmes to reduce gender disparities in business ownership and export activity.

The EU has made gender equality an explicit priority across different policy domains, including trade. Recent free trade agreements, for example, contain dedicated articles and chapters on trade and gender, signalling a shift towards a more systematic integration of gender considerations in EU trade policy (European Parliament, 2024[5]). On its side, the Czech national government has also adopted national gender strategies which include specific references to women entrepreneurship. For example, the "Gender Equality Strategy 2021-2030" highlights the importance of getting more women into entrepreneurship (Office of the Government of the Czech Republic, 2021[6]), while the specific scheme "Strengthening the Competencies of Women Disadvantaged in the Labour Market and in Business" (under the Operational Programme "Employment Plus") supports women over 50 through comprehensive educational programmes aiming to reduce the risk of poverty in retirement[5].

Building on these policy foundations, there is an opportunity for CzechTrade to further strengthen support for women entrepreneurs and women-led businesses in export activities. CzechTrade already organises a wide range of events tailored to different stages of export readiness and to region-specific market opportunities. Under Measure 11 of the National SME Support Strategy (i.e., Professional training for exporters), CzechTrade could expand its offer by introducing a targeted series of export training and networking activities specifically designed for women entrepreneurs.

Export alliances provide valuable expertise to many SMEs, but the sector coverage could be strengthened

CzechTrade is also active in the support of export alliances, which are sector-based collaborations aiming to enhance the international competitiveness of domestic firms by pooling expertise and resources. They offer services such as market intelligence, intellectual property guidance, and support for entering foreign markets. In Czechia, several export alliances were established in 2021 and 2022, including Elements for Smart Cities, the Czech Water Alliance, the PROVEG Czech Export Alliance, and the Czech Beer Alliance.

Broadening export alliances to new sectors and strengthening the role of the promoters of these alliances would enhance the visibility of this policy and would encourage wider SME engagement. Furthermore, consolidating selected alliances into formal export consortia could reinforce medium- and long-term strategic collaborations, without requiring participating firms to relinquish ownership (see Box 3.2).

Box 3.2. Italy's export consortia

The Italian government has a long tradition in supporting export consortia. These are voluntary alliances of SMEs, which come together to improve their export performance through the development of common activities. Each consortium needs to have at least eight SMEs (five in southern Italy). A consortium grant is worth on average EUR 2-3 million per year and funds are primarily used to finance visits abroad, workshops and advertising. Grants are disbursed annually, based on the expenses incurred in the previous year. A maximum of 40% of promotional expenses (60% for consortia based in Southern Italy) can be funded through the grants.

There are over 300 export consortia currently operating in Italy, covering a variety of sectors and regions. These consortia collectively include around 7 000 Italian companies The Italian Federation of Export Consortia (Feder-export) – the private federation historically associated with export consortia – represents about 110 consortia. It provides tax and legal advice, organises conferences and market surveys, arranges trade delegations, and negotiates credit lines with banks to finance the export activities of the consortia. Not all export consortia receive public funding, but they can apply to a competitive selection process (see above).

Source: OECD (2014[7]), *Italy: Key Issues and Policies*, OECD Studies on SMEs and Entrepreneurship, OECD Publishing, Paris, https://doi.org/10.1787/9789264213951-en.

Many SMEs already benefit from participation in trade missions and economic diplomacy initiatives

CzechTrade also plays a central role in facilitating export support services for SMEs, including market research, matchmaking, and organising participation in trade missions. In 2022 alone, slightly more than 1 000 companies across various sectors benefited from its services. CzechTrade also implements several EU-co-financed economic diplomacy programmes.

For example, NOVUMM (i.e., New Marketing Models for Trade Fair Participation) is an export support initiative implemented by CzechTrade to help SMEs enter and strengthen their presence into foreign markets. The programme provides subsidised services that make it easier and more affordable for SMEs to participate in foreign trade fairs, exhibitions, and international events. Rather than receiving direct grants, participating companies benefit from reduced-price export promotion services which are co-ordinated by CzechTrade. Under the original NOVUMM projects, nearly 1 400 SMEs were supported to participate in 167 trade fairs in 23 different countries. In the current programming period, through the Operational Programme "Technology and Applications for Competitiveness" (OP TAC), these efforts continue through the follow-up projects NOVUMM 2 and NOVUMM2KET. The former focuses on facilitating SME participation into selected international trade shows, while the latter targets specialised events in key technology sectors.

Alongside CzechTrade, the Czech Chamber of Commerce also plays a role in the field of trade missions and economic diplomacy, offering services similar to those of CzechTrade (e.g., information on market conditions, facilitating connections with international partners, and enabling participation in global events).

The export destinations of the PROPEA programme could be expanded to foster export diversification

The PROPEA programme is an important tool of economic diplomacy. It was successfully developed in 2022, with the participation of 16 embassies. As part of the project, participating embassies support Czech companies in entering the target foreign market through the services of accredited local experts, including support with the development of business plans, regulatory analysis and marketing of the company in the market destination, all of this based on a commercial contractual relationship between the Czech company and the foreign representative.

While the current portfolio of PROPEA services appears to be comprehensive, future support could be developed and extended to include more destinations. This approach would align with the goal of the National Export Strategy, which aims to diversify national exports beyond traditional markets and to assist SMEs in selecting new export destinations.

Stronger FDI-SME linkages could be supported through an expansion of information tools and new supplier development programmes

Czechia mainly supports FDI-SME linkages through the provision of financial incentives and technical assistance (OECD, 2024[1]). Current technical support tools to strengthen FDI-SME linkages are managed by the national Investment Promotion Agency CzechInvest and include a Czech supplier database featuring over 3 600 companies, many of which are SMEs. Active since 1998, the database categorises suppliers into ten key sectors with further subcategories, under which SMEs can register for free. The database is widely used by MNEs across Europe and beyond, particularly in sectors such as electrical engineering, automotive, ICT, metal subcontracting, and general engineering. The supplier database is a well-functioning and accessible tool that could be further expanded. Above all, the government could consider integrating CzechInvest's supplier database with other similar initiatives, like the Exporter's Directory of CzechTrade, into one single database, in order to build stronger visibility for foreign companies and buyers (OECD, 2024[1]).

In this area, there is also an opportunity to enhance the capabilities of local suppliers. This is particularly relevant for FDI-driven sectors with high growth potential, such as electronics and semiconductors. The Czech government had operated a supplier development programme (SDP) between 2000 and 2008, with a focus on fostering linkages between inward FDI and local SMEs particularly in the electronics and automotive sectors. The programme was demand-driven and focused on enhancing the competitiveness of Czech SMEs to meet the standards needed to integrate the GVCs as suppliers of the multinational companies (World Bank/WEF, n.d.[8]). Overall, the programme was highly effective, with approximately

150 participating companies, primarily SMEs, securing contracts with MNEs worth over CZK 7 billion until 2008.

Although the programme was discontinued after 2008, the government is currently preparing a new SDP under the National Semiconductor Strategy, covering the 2024-2029 period. In this context, the Czech government could consider establishing a broader SDP that extends beyond semiconductors to additional strategic sectors, in order to strengthen supplier–buyer linkages across a wider part of the national economy. SDPs provide local SMEs with valuable opportunities to network with MNEs and enhance their competitiveness by diversifying their product offerings and client base. These programmes typically provide SMEs with technical expertise to improve their product quality standards and facilitate their transformation from serving only one main multinational company into more independent suppliers. Introducing SDPs other strategic sectors with high entry barriers would align well with the Czech National Export Strategy and would complement existing support measures, such as SME consulting services and participation in international trade fairs, which are designed to help Czech SMEs become exporters of high-value final products and services.

Supply chain finance could be encouraged to strengthen the liquidity of SMEs

In the context of GVCs, there is also scope for improving the financing ecosystem around buyer-supplier relationships through the development of supply chain finance (SCF). SCF refers to a set of financial solutions that optimise cash flow along a supply chain by enabling suppliers to receive early payment on their invoices (with a discount factor), while allowing buyers to extend their payment terms without impacting the liquidity of suppliers. Given that 61% of Czech companies experience late payments as against 43% at the EU level (OECD, 2024[1]), SCF can be an effective solution to address this issue by enabling SMEs to receive early payments through third-party providers.

In line with the EU Capital Markets Union Action Plan *(*see Chapter 2 on Access to Finance*)*, as well as with the Recommendation of the OECD Council on SME Financing, Czechia could explore different options to enhance SME access to SFC, such as regulatory measures to incentivise buyers to adopt shorter payment terms for suppliers, simplification of SCF documentation, awareness raising and technical support measures such training on e-invoicing, and the development of e-platforms for SCF solutions.

Box 3.3. SME internationalisation policies from an EU legislation perspective

Czechia has made progress in the implementation of a variety of measures to support trade facilitation in the EU Single Market. These include measures set out in the "Long-term Action Plan for the Better Implementation and Enforcement of Single-Market Rules", as well as the implementation of the Single Digital Gateway. Other export support services building on European initiatives and used by Czech SMEs include the "Access2Markets" portal, the Point of Single Contact, SOLVIT, and the Product Contact Point, which have been discussed in the first part of this chapter, and which help SMEs effectively navigate the EU Single Market.

Additional services that help SMEs become export-ready are available in Czechia through the **Enterprise Europe Network (EEN),** which is also co-funded by the EU. Among other things, the network provides advisory services and innovation support to guide SMEs on their way to export products or services to new markets.

Finally, as highlighted in the annual implementation plans of the National SME Support Strategy, Czech SMEs benefit from the existing Free Trade Agreements (FTAs) between the EU and third-country partners, including Canada, Japan, Chile, and New Zealand. In this respect, there is an opportunity to build on the gender provisions of FTAs, such as those included in the recent EU-Chile agreement, to enhance support for women entrepreneurs in export activities through dedicated events. These measures would also align with Czechia's Gender Equality Strategy for 2021–2030, which intends to promote greater gender equality in international trade.

Conclusions and policy recommendations

The Czech economy is highly export-oriented, with exports accounting for 72% of GDP in 2023, the 12th highest value within the EU. While Czechia's export landscape is dominated by large MNEs, SME export volumes grew by 30% between 2012 and 2022. However, the number of SME exporters has remained stable, highlighting the need to increase export readiness among a larger group of SMEs.

The objectives and proposed actions of the Czech SME Support Strategy are aligned with those of the National Export Strategy and focus on the export readiness of SMEs, high-value-added exports, and building a stabler presence in foreign markets. Current major initiatives include the export incubators, the export alliances, information platforms and training courses, and trade missions and economic diplomacy initiatives. Some of the current measures could benefit from broader sectoral and geographical outreach, as well as an improved inclusion of underrepresented groups in export activities like women entrepreneurs. Finally, further strengthening FDI-SME linkages and promoting supply-chain finance solutions can support the indirect participation of local SMEs in foreign markets through participation in global value chains. In doing so, these policies will increase the Czech value-added in national exports, which is currently relatively low.

Against this backdrop, the following recommendations are put forward to enhance the internationalisation of Czech SMEs:

- Increase visibility and simplify access to export information for SMEs (in line with the "no wrong door" principle), for example, by developing a comprehensive document that gives an overview of relevant tools, training programmes, and export financing options for SME exporters.
- Establish a series of dedicated export training and networking events for entrepreneurs underrepresented in foreign markets, notably women, to boost their participation in international trade.
- Further support the creation of export alliances and export consortia to enable SMEs with similar products or distribution channels to easily access foreign markets at lower cost.
- Expand the network of export destinations within the PROPEA (Projects for the Support of Economic Activities Abroad) programme to maximise global coverage of available export services.
- Re-establish and further develop supplier development programmes to strengthen the linkages between local SMEs and foreign MNEs, particularly in highly internationalised and high-growth sectors such as electronics and semiconductors.
- Promote the use of supply-chain finance (SCF) solutions by SMEs and larger buyers, including through regulatory measures to incentivise large buyers to adopt shorter payment terms for small suppliers, simplification of SCF documentation, awareness raising and training, and the development of web platforms for SCF solutions.

References

AMSP, CEB, EGAP, KP, IPSOS (2023), *Export of Small and Medium Sized Companies*, https://www.amsp.cz/media/amsp/3833/export-62023-final.pdf. [10]

EGAP (2024), *Annual Report 2023*, https://www.egap.cz/en/annual-reports. [9]

European Parliament (2024), *Gender mainstreaming in EU trade agreements*, https://www.europarl.europa.eu/thinktank/en/document/EPRS_BRI(2024)760388. [5]

López González, J. (2017), "Mapping the participation of ASEAN small- and medium- sized enterprises in global value chains", *OECD Trade Policy Papers*, No. 203, OECD Publishing, Paris, https://doi.org/10.1787/2dc1751e-en. [3]

Ministry of Industry and Trade (MIT), Czechia (2023), *Annual Implementation Report 2023 of the SME Support Strategy*. [11]

OECD (2024), *Strengthening FDI and SME Linkages in Czechia*, OECD Publishing, Paris, https://doi.org/10.1787/4c97d104-en. [1]

OECD (2021), *SME and Entrepreneurship Policy in the Slovak Republic*, OECD Studies on SMEs and Entrepreneurship, OECD Publishing, Paris, https://doi.org/10.1787/9097a251-en. [2]

OECD (2014), *Italy: Key Issues and Policies*, OECD Studies on SMEs and Entrepreneurship, OECD Publishing, Paris, https://doi.org/10.1787/9789264213951-en. [7]

OECD/European Commission (2023), *The Missing Entrepreneurs 2023: Policies for Inclusive Entrepreneurship and Self-Employment*, OECD Publishing, Paris, https://doi.org/10.1787/230efc78-en. [4]

Office of the Government of the Czech Republic (2021), *Gender Equality Strategy for 2021 – 2030*, https://vlada.gov.cz/assets/ppov/gcfge/Gender-Equality-Strategy-2021-2030.pdf. [6]

World Bank/WEF (n.d.), *Pilot Czech Supplier Development Programme in Eleectronics and Automotive*, https://www3.weforum.org/docs/Manufacturing_Our_Future_2016/Case_Study_13.pdf. [8]

Notes

[1] It should be noted that "export as a percentage of GDP" is an indicator also influenced by the size of a country. The larger a country, the larger its domestic market and, as a result, the lower the share of exports in national GDP, all else being equal.

[2] Based on information from the "Annual Implementation Report 2023" of the SME Support Strategy, provided by Czechia's Ministry of Industry and Trade (MIT).

[3] Source: OECD Data Explorer: Trade in goods by enterprise characteristics by economic activity and size class.

[4] In automotive, for example, high value-added activities in precision manufacturing include the robotic welding of car bodies and assembling transmissions, while quality assurance includes vehicle testing (e.g. breaking, emissions, etc.) and traceability systems.

[5] Further information on the Operational Programme "Employment Plus" is available here: https://eurydice.eacea.ec.europa.eu/national-education-systems/czechia/national-reforms-related-adult-education-and-training.

4 SME skills development and entrepreneurship skills

Workforce skills upgrading is key for companies of any size to remain competitive in the face of rapidly evolving technologies. In Czechia, the share of adults participating in training activities is lower than the EU average, which may slow down the adaptation of the labour force to new skills demands, while the share of STEM graduates is slightly higher than the OECD average. One of the main skills policies of the Czech government has involved strengthening the digital skills of workers, notably through different project calls of the national Recovery and Resilience Plan (RRP) and of two different Operational Programmes. Czechia also features a growing offer of micro-credentials, which are short-term courses addressing specific skills needs, while greater efforts are needed to strengthen the awareness of employers about "recognition of prior learning". With regard to entrepreneurship skills, the national entrepreneurship ecosystem has developed significantly in the last years, although the overall quality of institutions like business incubators and accelerators is heterogeneous. On the other hand, the offer of entrepreneurship education is still at an incipient stage, despite the existence of some good practices at both secondary and tertiary levels.

Key messages

- Workforce skills upgrading is key for companies, regardless of their size, to stay competitive in the face of rapidly evolving technologies. **In Czechia, however, a smaller share of adults than the EU average participate in training activities**. This is partly the result of low unemployment, which makes the need for training less immediate, but in the long run it may hinder the adaptation of the labour force to new skills demands. In a similar vein, although the number of Science, Technology, Engineering and Mathematics (STEM) graduates has steadily increased since 2017, the demand for these skills is expected to outpace its supply.
- **One of the mains skills policy priorities of the Czech government has involved strengthening the digital skills of the workforce**. For example, the employment component of the national Recovery and Resilience Plan (RRP) aims to upskill 130 000 people on IT skills and Industry 4.0 skills by the end of 2025. Specific interventions include an e-shop providing workers with access to subsidised training and the programme "NPO-DIGI for Companies", which directly supports enterprises which wish to invest in the digital training of their workforces. The Operational Programme Employment Plus (OPE+), which is managed by the Ministry of Labour and Social Affairs, also has several calls to upskill workers, including one dedicated to enhancing the entrepreneurial competencies of senior workers.
- "Recognition of prior learning" allows individuals to receive a formal accreditation for skills that have been acquired outside traditional educational channels. In doing so, it helps reduce skills mismatches, avoid unnecessary (formal) training, and improve business productivity. In Czechia, **although the recognition of prior learning is guaranteed by Law 179/2006, employers are little aware of it**, pointing to the importance of more awareness-raising efforts in the future.
- **Czechia also displays a growing offer of micro-credentials, which are short-term courses to address very specific skills needs**. Micro-credentials are especially important at a time when skills demand changes rapidly due to evolving digital technologies and when this often entails the development of new skills in existing jobs rather than the full development of new professional occupations. While the main providers of micro-credentials are generally vocational and technical institutes, some Czech universities have also experimented with this offer, including as a means to attract students into longer education courses.
- **Czechia's entrepreneurial ecosystem has evolved rapidly in the last decade**. CzechInvest, which is the investment agency of Czechia, but which has increasingly engaged in start-up support, is the main government player in the national entrepreneurship ecosystem, which also includes other institutions like universities and private entities. **Nonetheless, the overall quality of the entrepreneurship ecosystem is heterogenous**. Half of the existing business incubators/accelerators are not active, and another sizeable share only offers online/remote services.
- **The offer of entrepreneurship education is at an initial stage in Czechia, although there are some interesting initiatives** both at secondary (e.g., "fictitious company" programme) and tertiary levels (e.g., Brno's Moravian Innovation Centre). Measures to strengthen this offer could include developing entrepreneurship education courses in tertiary institutions that already have an incubator, to ensure progression in the entrepreneurial journey of students, and developing a national entrepreneurship education curriculum to be applied more consistently to entrepreneurship teaching across secondary and tertiary education.

Workforce skills and education in Czechia

The digital and green transition will have a major impact on the national labour market

The twin transition, green and digital, is expected to have a major impact on labour market needs and skills requirements. Across OECD countries, it is estimated that between 2015 and 2019, on average, 20% of the workforce was already employed in green-task jobs. By contrast, "brown" industries accounted for only 7% of employment, but workers in these sectors face the risk of job loss and prolonged periods of unemployment without supporting employment policies (OECD, 2024[1]).

The twin transition will require important upskilling and reskilling investments for companies to remain competitive and grow. For example, a survey conducted on the impact of Artificial Intelligence (AI) on the workplace shows that 71% of employers in manufacturing across OECD countries have already retrained their workers due to AI (Lane, Williams and Broecke, 2023[2]). In addition, recent studies show that at least 40% of the workforce will need upskilling and reskilling, as rapidly evolving technologies such as generative AI, machine learning, and advanced manufacturing emerge (World Economic Forum, 2023[3]). The skills gap that small and medium enterprises (SMEs) typically experience might also widen, as SME workers are generally less involved in formal and non-formal training activities than those in larger companies. According to the latest available data, adult participation in formal job-related learning is on average 15 percentage points lower in SMEs than in large companies at the EU level (OECD, 2019[4]).

Czechia's economy has traditionally been manufacturing-based and export-oriented (see also chapter 3), although more recently there have been signs that the services sector, especially the ICT sector, is gaining traction. Both sectors will be heavily impacted by recent digital trends, transforming jobs and skills requirements. Robot intensity in Czechia's manufacturing industry has increased considerably since 2005[1], thus boosting demand for digital skills. However, automation does not only concern manufacturing. Estimates by Czech authorities suggest that over the next 30 years automation could affect more than 50% of professional tasks across the entire economy, impacting 3.4 million people at the national level (Ministry of Industry and Trade of Czechia, 2022[5]).

Artificial intelligence will also reinforce the demand for advanced digital and transversal skills. Sectors that use generative AI to improve efficiency are expected to prioritise transversal skills such as creativity, problem solving, and critical thinking, as the capacity to lead and use advanced technologies will depend on human adaptability and oversight (Borgonovi et al., 2023[6]).

The number of adults in training has grown, but greater attention is needed to the development of transversal skills

Against this backdrop, over the last decade, the European Union has seen an upward trend in adult participation in further education. While Czechia initially followed this trend, participation declined between 2017 and 2020 before experiencing a sharp increase and reaching 9.9% in 2023. This is higher than neighbouring countries such as Poland and Germany but still below the EU average (Figure 4.1, Panel A). When looking at training participation by different professional categories, Czechia scores below the EU average across almost all categories, but especially so for managers and professionals, suggesting that more efforts are needed to upskill and reskill these groups (Figure 4.1, Panel B). In this regard, recent data show that continuous vocational training lacks a focus on transversal skills such as problem solving, customer handling, teamwork, and office administration, which are skills especially relevant for professionals and managers[2].

Figure 4.1. Participation of adults in training in Czechia

Percentage values

Panel A: Share of adults participating in training in the previous four weeks for selected EU countries, 2014-2023	Panel B: Participation rate of employees in education and training by occupation

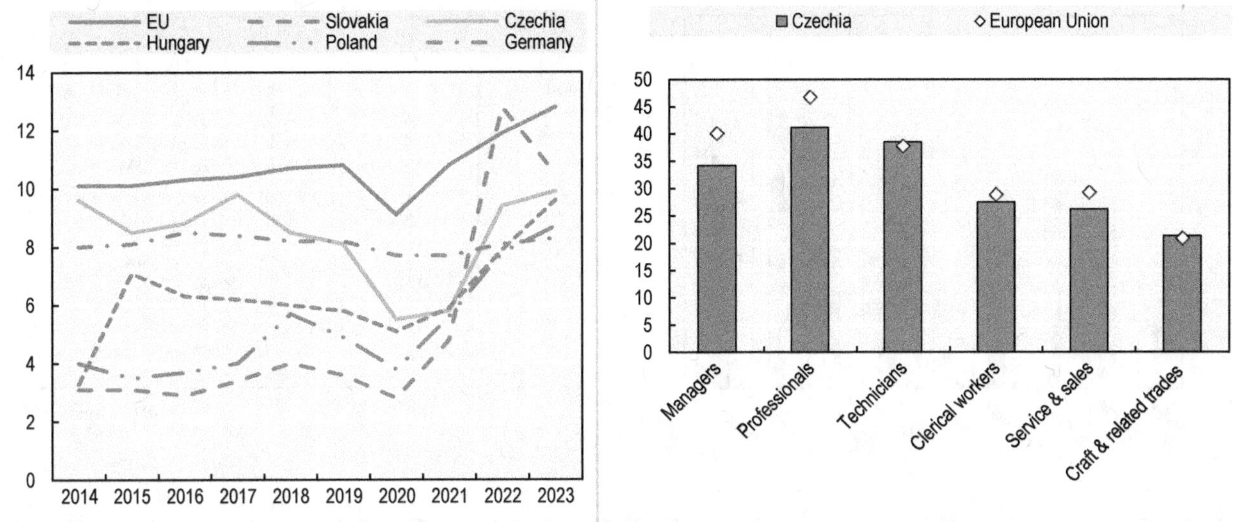

Note: For Panel B the classification of occupations is based on the International Standard Classification of Occupations (ISCO) of the International Labour Organisation, Managers and Professional are the most skilled workers. Professionals do not necessarily have a managerial role but distinguish themselves from technicians or clerical workers by their high level of competencies. Professionals include engineers, chemists, mathematicians, medical doctors, teaching professionals, business, and administration professionals.
Source: Panel A Eurostat 2023 based on EU Labour force Survey Data; Panel B Eurostat 2022 based on Continuous Vocational Training Survey (CVTS).

With respect to digital skills, in 2023, about one-quarter of Czech businesses (23%) trained their staff in ICT skills, slightly better than the EU average (22%) and neighbouring countries like Hungary and Slovakia (18% and 15%), but worse than Poland (25%) (Eurostat, 2023[7]) (Figure 4.2, Panel A). SMEs are less likely to provide ICT training to their workers: in Czechia, only 16% of SMEs offered ICT-relevant training to their employees, slightly below the EU average (18%), but above Slovakia and Hungary (Figure 4.2, Panel B).

Figure 4.2. Enterprises training their employees with ICT skills

Percentage values

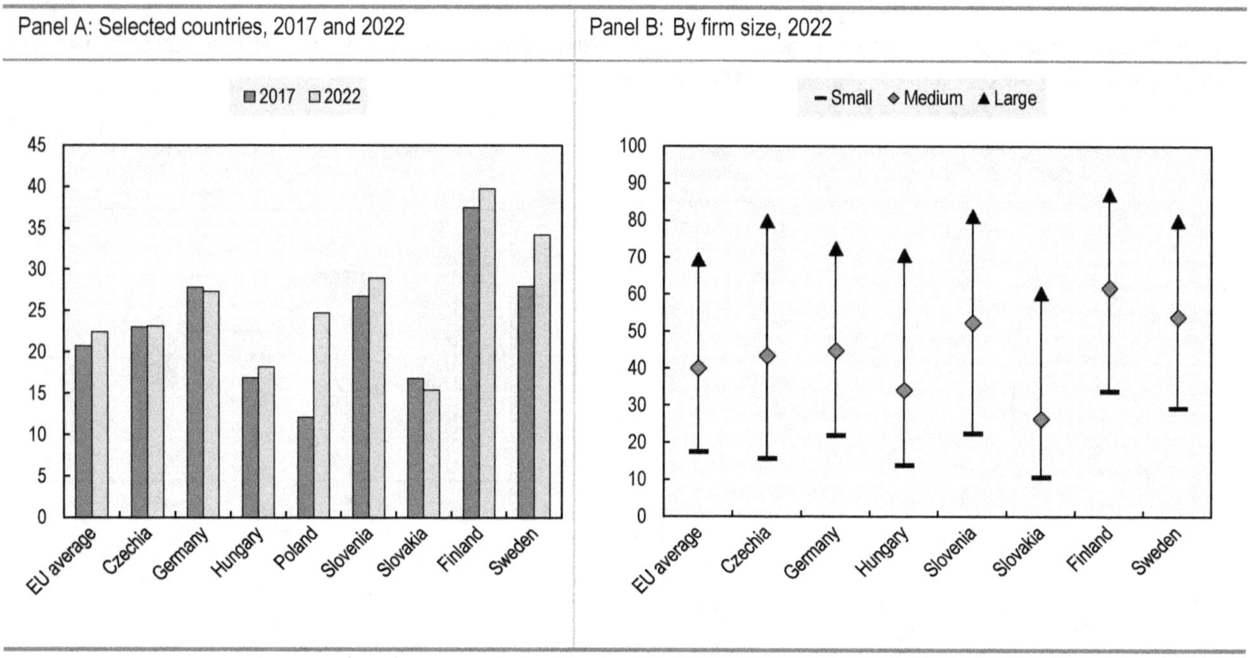

Source: Eurostat 2022

The number of graduates is on the rise, including in STEM subjects, but this might not be enough to match expected future demand

Czechia is home to 26 public universities. The country has a growing share of bachelor's and master's graduates in the field of ICT, accounting for 5.1% of total graduates in 2021. The number of graduates in Science, Technology, Engineering and Mathematics (STEM) has also steadily increased since 2017, reaching 25% of the total in 2021, slightly above the OECD average of 23.7% (OECD, 2024[8]).

Despite the relatively high number of graduates in STEM disciplines, there are signs that the offer of high-level qualifications must expand to prevent skills gaps in the future (Cedefop, 2023[9]). In 2022, 34.5% of Czech adults (aged 25-34) had completed tertiary education, which is one of the lowest rates in the EU. Furthermore, the share of adults (aged 25-64) with tertiary education was only 27% in 2023, lower than other Central and Eastern European (CEE) countries and the OECD average (41%) (OECD, 2023[10]).

SME and entrepreneurship skills policies: Mid-term evaluation of the national SME strategy

An amendment to the Employment Act has introduced more flexible working arrangements that should facilitate the uptake of vocational training

The Employment Act, which dates back to 1964, has recently been revised to introduce more flexible work arrangements. The amendment, effective as of October 2023, is the result of a year-long intensive dialogue with social partners and aims to introduce more flexible contractual arrangements, clarify rules for remote working, facilitate part-time employment, and support the re-integration of the inactive and unemployed into the labour market[3]. Most relevant for this chapter, this amendment makes it easier for workers to engage in vocational training and for companies to attract and hire skilled talent. For example, the facilitation of part-time employment allows workers to have more time to enrol in vocational training while maintaining their current occupation. Similarly, the amendment will make it easier for companies to recruit non-EU foreign workers.

Going forward, a further improvement would consist in a clear reference to lifelong learning as a career development objective, with the aim of ensuring that flexible work arrangements go hand in hand with training objectives (Chamber of Commerce of Czechia, 2024[11]).

Digital training interfaces provide simplified access to training

As part of the Recovery and Resilience Plan (RRP), the Ministry of Labour and Social Affairs has set up an e-shop providing workers with access to subsidised training courses. Any user can browse, select and enrol in courses via this e-shop. Courses fall under two categories: "retraining" in a specific technical field and digital education. Courses are delivered online, in person or in hybrid mode by recognised training institutions. Initially only available to the unemployed, these courses have more recently been made open also to employed people, who can spend up to CZK 50 000 (i.e., about EUR 2 000) in training courses within a three-year period. All applications are submitted online and are reviewed by the National Labour Office. As of July 2024, the e-shop had already supported nearly 19 000 people, of whom 11 000 were employees and 8 000 unemployed, and had involved around 500 learning institutions[4].

The training e-shop is just one element of a broader vocational training initiative, implemented under the Employment component of the RRP, which aims to upskill 130 000 learners in IT or Industry 4.0 skills by the end of 2025. This component also includes a digital education initiative – the "NPO-DIGI for Companies" – which is also managed by the Czech National Labour Office, and which allows companies to retrain their employees with digital skills. The programme offers grants to companies to cover either the direct costs of a training course or a wage subsidy for the hours that employees spend attending the course.

Both initiatives show the commitment of the Czech government to meet the upskilling and reskilling objectives outlined in the National SME Support strategy.

The Operational Programme "Employment Plus" has several calls to for the skills upgrading of the workforce

The Operational Programme Employment Plus (2021-2027) (OPE+) is the main government programme for employment and social inclusion. Co-ordinated by the Ministry of Labour and Social Affairs and funded by the European Social Fund Plus, it builds upon the achievements of the previous Operational Programme Employment (2014-2020). OPE+ aims to enhance employment opportunities, improve workforce adaptability, promote gender equality, and foster social inclusion. Unlike the Operational Programme Technology and Application for Competitiveness (OP TAC), managed by the Ministry of Industry and Trade (MIT), which focuses on helping firms to become more competitive through different means, including workforce training, OPE+ focuses on retraining workers and preparing them for the future of work.

A strong emphasis in OPE+ is placed on increasing participation in further education among senior workers (55-64 years old) and low-skilled adults, as these groups exhibit lower enrolment rates in further education. Targeted measures also include retraining and counselling workers in declining industries or in companies that are adopting low-carbon business models. To achieve these priorities, OPE+ has launched calls to finance several training activities, including courses on soft skills, management and languages, as well as the acquisition of new competences relevant for the green transition and Industry 4.0.

By way of example, in March 2023, a project call of OPE+ aimed to support employers in enhancing the business competencies of their employees, with a particular focus on senior workers (aged 55+). Eligible applicants included business enterprises, state-owned enterprises and self-employed individuals, while supported activities included courses in the areas of soft and managerial skills and language training. To participate in this call, employers were asked to submit their application electronically, and were required to specify target values for indicators, such as the total number of participants and the number of participants aged 55 and over. The project call closed in June 2023, but each selected project can run until May 2026 and receive funding between CZK 1-6 million.

This initiative stands out from other OPE+ calls for its focus on SMEs. Fostering soft skills (e.g., critical thinking, problem solving and adaptability) and managerial skills can help workers, especially senior ones, to navigate changes in the labour market and transition to new jobs and responsibilities. As such, this call responded directly to the objective of the national SME Support Strategy of "ensuring further education, especially in area of key skills". It also supported the objective of "increasing the level of digital skills in the business sector", as soft and managerial skills can help businesses adapt to new market conditions and implement new disruptive digital technologies more swiftly.

Another call of OPE+, launched in July 2023, has supported employees at risk of redundancy, including in companies transitioning to lower-carbon business models. More specifically, this call provided the National Labour Office with resources to design and implement programmes supporting employees in companies going through restructuring. Benefitting from a financial allocation of CZK 300 million (EUR 11.9 million), the National Labour Office designed different activities such as retraining opportunities for employees facing the loss of employment, the delivery of professional qualification exams, career counselling and job placement services. The support also included wage subsidies for employers during employee participation in training. This call closed in November 2025, with projects required to be completed by December 2028.

By targeting companies in sectors in transition, this initiative stands out as one of the few Czech government programmes aiming to prepare workers who might be at risk of losing their jobs because of external shocks. Similar measures can be found in other countries such as Portugal with "*Qualifica Industria*" (Qualify Industry), a training programme launched in September 2023 for industrial companies facing a decrease in production due to unexpected market conditions. However, the Czech scheme targets directly workers, not companies, and provides additional services such as career counselling or direct job placement of workers.

As of end-2024, as these calls were still open, no evaluation had been undertaken to assess the uptake or the impact of these programmes. However, to obtain feedback on the OPE+ calls, the Ministry of Labour and Social Affairs undertook a survey at the end of 2023. The survey revealed that 85% of respondents were satisfied with the management of the calls, with 25% fully satisfied and 60% rather satisfied. However, 27% found the administrative burden heavier than expected, particularly new applicants. Furthermore, 23% of respondents reported difficulties with the software used for application. While 90% of successful applicants found the evaluation of their application justified, only 48% of unsuccessful applicants agreed. Satisfaction with transparency of the selection process was expectedly higher among successful applicants (92%) than among unsuccessful ones (50%). Furthermore, most respondents reported that the length of the evaluation process was in line with their expectations, and many were satisfied with the support offered by the contact point of the Ministry of Labour and Social Affairs.

There are some government initiatives to improve the quality of teaching and to connect schools to companies

In line with the National SME Support Strategy, Czech schools have been provided with modern IT equipment (e.g., new computers, interactive whiteboards, etc.) enabling more efficient and personalised teaching and learning experiences. For instance, the integration of videos, graphics, and interactive simulations offers different ways of presenting information, making complex topics easier to understand and allowing for more participatory approaches to learning, which can in turn enhance key skills such as problem solving, critical thinking and communication. These reforms are a step in the right direction towards training the workforce of the future[5].

Furthermore, the Operational Programme "Johannes Amos Comenius" (JAC), managed by the Ministry of Education, actively supports collaboration between educational institutions and employers. This is evident in two calls targeting primary and secondary schools, with a combined budget of CZK 11 billion. In primary schools, the focus is on career counselling. In secondary schools, including vocational schools, the initiative extends to both career counselling and fostering connections between students and companies, including SMEs. The first two calls were launched in 2022, and two follow-up calls in 2024. For the call connecting secondary schools to companies, activities include internships, company tours, as well as support for the creation of "fictitious companies" (i.e., teaching pupils on how to create a business plan and produce a tangible product or services)[6].

This last programme is especially relevant. Connecting students in secondary and vocational education to companies provides valuable real-world experience, helping students apply classroom knowledge and develop essential skills. It also enhances their career awareness and employability by exposing them to various industries and creating networking opportunities. Finally, engaging high school pupils in entrepreneurial projects, even if just for pedagogical purposes, can help foster a new generation of entrepreneurs and workers who have transversal skills, such as problem solving, creativity and critical thinking (see section below). For companies, these initiatives provide access to a future pool of talent, strengthen the company's reputation within the community, and can lead to long-term partnerships with educational institutions. As of mid-2024, a large number of SMEs had enrolled in the OP JAC call.

The Czech law formally recognises prior learning, but awareness among employers is still low

The recognition of prior learning allows individuals to gain formal credit (qualifications and certifications) for skills and knowledge that they have already acquired through work or other life experiences outside traditional education, thus reducing the time and cost needed to achieve qualifications (Meghnagi and Tuccio, 2022[12]). The recognition of prior learning acknowledges that individuals can acquire skills through work, volunteering, workshops and other means, making learning more accessible and socially inclusive. Recognition of prior learning is especially beneficial for SMEs, as it enables companies to quickly identify and utilise the available skills of their workers, thus reducing the need for extensive training.

In Czechia, every citizen has the right to have their skills and knowledge assessed under Act Number 179 of 2006, which governs the verification and recognition of lifelong learning outcomes. This law covers 1 451 professional qualifications, and a successful assessments result in an official certificate. To date, more than 300 000 individuals in Czechia have obtained a certification through this process, and a web portal has been created to validate non-formal learning in different fields.

Nonetheless, the awareness of employers of this law is still low and could be strengthened, with a view to having the skills of SME workers better recognised in their current employment and to reducing skills mismatches not only at the firm level, but also in the wider labour market.

Micro-credentials, currently being developed, are an important short-term solution for the rapid development of practical skills

Another important development in Czechia concerns the delivery of practice-oriented micro-credentials, a trend that has also gained traction in other OECD countries. In Czechia, supported by the national RRP, twenty-six universities, including prestigious institutions such as the Charles University in Prague, have introduced micro-credential programmes. The business community is generally supportive of this development, as these certificates equip students and workers with business-relevant skills in a relatively short period of time. For both employers and workers who do not have time to engage in long learning activities, a short programme that provides valuable skills is an asset for professional mobility and development[7].

While companies are generally supportive, universities are often less prepared to offering micro-credentials. A change in this direction often requires a certain degree of adaptability, including the training of faculty members in business-relevant topics and in the digital infrastructure through which these courses are typically delivered. Many universities struggle to adapt to this new type of training, also due to concerns about favouring vocational training over traditional education and penalising disciplines that foster critical thinking but have little immediate market value (Varadarajan, Koh and Daniel, 2023[13]). Furthermore, in this specific area, universities often face steep competition from other organisations, such as community colleges or even employers (Cathles and Navarro, 2019[14]) (Ministry of Industry and Trade of Czechia, 2022[5]). This has led some universities to use micro-credentials as a hook to attract people into enrolling into more traditional education programmes.

CzechInvest is the main government player in the field of business incubation and acceleration support

Czechia is home to a dynamic and growing start-up ecosystem, with several hubs across the country. (Keiretsu Forum, 2020[15]) (Atomico, Google for Start-ups, 2022[16]).[8] In terms of government support, CzechInvest, the national investment agency, has progressively become the main government player for entrepreneurship development. Although the original mission of the agency was to attract FDI, it has gradually diversified its activities to also serve the local entrepreneurship ecosystem. Leveraging its expertise on foreign trade, CzechInvest's first programme for start-ups (i.e., the "CzechAccelerator"), w launched in 2011, aimed to help young ventures to grow and enter foreign markets through connections with some of the top global business accelerators. The programme also helped start-ups to meet foreign mentors and to participate in trade fairs and conferences. In 2016, CzechInvest launched a follow-up project called "Startup Support", along similar lines to the CzechAccelerator. As of mid-2024, 395 start-ups had received support from CzechInvest through this programme, and 5 new start-ups undertake internationalisation activities every month.

Beyond helping companies to internationalise, CzechInvest supports start-up development through business incubation services in strategic sectors identified by the National Research and Innovation Strategy for Smart Specialisation of Czechia 2021–2027 (hereafter the "RIS3 strategy"). These include mobility innovation, creative industries, space, and cutting-edge digital fields such as advanced technology and materials, eco-technology, artificial intelligence, and "tech4life" (technology to improve quality of life). Funded by the Ministry of Industry and Trade, the "Technology Incubation" programme has a duration of two years and provides direct funding to selected technology start-ups (up to CZK 4.5 million, i.e., EUR 180 000 euros). Indirect (conditional) funding of up to CZK 500 000 (i.e., EUR 20 000) is also provided for advisory services (consultation with business and technology experts), as well as workshops, seminars, and networking events to connect start-ups to potential financiers.

Many other institutions, including universities, are actively involved in the entrepreneurial ecosystem

Besides the accelerators and incubators of CzechInvest, other innovation infrastructures (accelerators, incubators, co-working spaces, science and technology parks, digital innovation hubs) have developed over the last years with the support of EU and national funding. An online survey covering the period 2019-2020, with 150 responding start-ups, found that 66% of them had participated in an acceleration programme, almost twice the proportion in the 2017-2018 period (Keiretsu Forum, 2020[15]).

In particular, Czech universities host accelerators and incubators that are open to students and local start-ups. For example, the Technical University of Ostrava hosts one of the most important incubation and acceleration programme in the Moravian-Silesian region, "the Green Light" programme, which was established in 2014 and is open to all students and entrepreneurs from the region. It includes the "start track" for business ideation and the "accelerator track" for business scale-up. Both tracks include consultations, mentoring and networking events, but the accelerator offers more advanced workshops teaching entrepreneurs about marketing, finance, business plan and legal matters, as well as networking events with investors.

The Czech Technical University in Prague also set up an incubator programme in 2020, with the support of the Ministry of Education, Youth and Sports. The incubator, called "InQbay", is open to students, PhD candidates, entrepreneurs and university employees. Its support includes counselling, mentoring, coaching and expert workshops, mostly aimed at the development of soft skills such as critical thinking and problem solving.

These two programmes are aligned with best practices in terms of incubations and acceleration support. They are not only open to university students and faculty, but also to surrounding start-ups, and are based on a competitive process which assesses the business model and market prospects of the supported entrepreneurs. One possible improvement, however, concerns the accelerator track of the Green Light programme, which does not have a sunset clause for participants – participants can attend the accelerator, within the limit of once a week, for as long as they want – whereas such clauses are typically important to encourage companies to find external investors and solutions to grow more quickly and to leave the comfort zone of government-supported services.

The quality of incubation and acceleration services is quite heterogeneous

A recent mapping of innovation infrastructures in Czechia, undertaken as a guiding tool to support the implementation of the national RIS3 strategy, revealed some weaknesses in the existing incubator and accelerator support system (Samek, 2022[17]). In particular, it found that while there were around 350 of these entities in Czechia in 2022, half of which public and the other half privately funded, only half of the total was really active. Furthermore, almost a quarter of the active incubators were virtual, providing only remote services and mentoring, while many other non-virtual incubators only provided basic infrastructure (e.g., office space), lacking more advanced technological infrastructure or training services such as open-access workshops. Finally, only few offered tax or accounting advice, which are also important in the stage of business creation and development.

The provision of entrepreneurship education could be further expanded

Beyond entrepreneurship support through business incubation and acceleration services, entrepreneurial skills and attitudes can also be taught and learned. Entrepreneurial skills not only empower individuals to start their own businesses but also enhance their leadership, creativity, critical thinking, and risk tolerance. These soft skills are often referred to as the "entrepreneurial mindset" and can be useful in many different work environments beyond entrepreneurship (Bacigalupo et al., 2016[18]).

As a result, many countries have introduced entrepreneurship teaching activities, mainly at the tertiary level of education targeting students from different academic disciplines. For example, in Sweden, the University of Linkoping has a dedicated course on entrepreneurship for PhD students ("Entrepreneurship in Theory and Practice") that supports students in the development of business ideas linked to their research programme. The programme also includes coaching and networking activities, has led to the creation of over 20 start-ups since 2006, and has attracted CZK 15 million in capital (Klofsten, Jones-Evans and Pereira, 2020[19]) (OECD/IDB, 2022[20]).

In Czechia, the tertiary education system offers entrepreneurship education, but the curriculum could be further expanded. One of the most noteworthy initiatives is the University of Ostrava's summer school of entrepreneurship education ("Entrepreneurship for All"), which is a three-week programme to help students launch their start-ups and includes courses on creativity and business creation, as well as field visits to local start-ups. In addition, the JIC Innovation Centre in Brno, in partnership with three local universities, offers semestral courses for undergraduates on entrepreneurship and business plan competitions to hone the entrepreneurial abilities of students. JIC has also created a PhD academy to bridge the gap between research and the market, helping students to connect their research to market needs.

While these examples are in line with good practices at the international level, more could be done to support the development of entrepreneurship education in Czechia, especially at the tertiary level. For example, offering entrepreneurship education in universities where there is already an incubator/accelerator could ease the emergence of a strong entrepreneurial pipeline. Memorial University in Newfoundland & Labrador, Canada, offers an example of this "interconnected approach". This university offers entrepreneurship teaching to bachelor's and master's students and has established entrepreneurship centres, incubators and accelerators. All these institutions are interconnected, meaning that students who follow courses on entrepreneurship can eventually join one of the start-up activities to continue their entrepreneurial journey (OECD, 2023[21]).

A more ambitious option would involve launching a national entrepreneurship education programme, which would entail the development of a national curriculum for entrepreneurship education. By embedding entrepreneurship education more systematically at a national level, governments can ensure consistent exposure to essential skills such as creativity, critical thinking, problem solving, risk taking, and financial literacy from an early age, all of which are key skills regardless of the future careers of pupils and students. For example, Finland integrates entrepreneurship education across all levels of education, from primary to tertiary level. The national core curriculum emphasises entrepreneurial learning, project-based learning, and co-operation with local businesses.

Box 4.1. SME and entrepreneurship skills policies from an EU legislation perspective

Since 2020, the European Commission has put forward a series of policy initiatives to guide member states and mobilise private-sector support for skills development, including for SMEs. The SME Strategy for a Sustainable and Digital Europe recognises the essential role of SMEs for EU competitiveness, noting that in 2020 a quarter of them reported struggling with the availability of skilled staff and experienced managers (European Commission, 2020[22]). Accordingly, one of the three pillars of the Strategy focuses on "building capacity" in SMEs to help them navigate the green and digital transition.

This pillar is implemented through the *Enterprise Europe Network* (EEN) and a network of European Digital Innovation Hubs (EDIHs). In Czechia, the Technology Centre of Prague, an association of public research institutes, co-ordinates the national EEN activities in collaboration with regional partners. The network, co-funded by the EU and the Czech Ministry of Industry and Trade, provides advisory services on management improvement, intellectual property rights and broader innovation capacity-building, including advice on marketing technologies and accessing European funding programmes. The European SME Strategy has also led to the creation of a network of 240 EIDHs, with hubs in every region of Europe. Six of these hubs have been set-up in Czechia, each with a different focus (see chapter 6 of this report for more details).

In July 2020, the European Commission launched the New European Skills Agenda (2020-2025), which set objectives for upskilling and reskilling to be achieved by 2025 and a 12-point action plan calling on Members States, companies and social partners to invest in skills development. The agenda aims to increase adult participation in learning to at least half of the EU population by 2025, with a particular focus on adults with low qualifications. It places special emphasis on basic digital skills, with a target of 70% of the EU adult population equipped with such skills and highlights the importance of green skills. In line with the Skills Agenda, the Council of the European Union adopted in 2022 two recommendations to strengthen lifelong learning: i) on individual learning accounts, encouraging Member States to set up accounts enabling easier access to training; ii) on a European approach to micro-credentials, paving the way for the expansion of short, tailored learning experiences that can be certified and recognised (Council of the European Union, 2022[23]) (Council of the European Union, 2022[24]).

Czechia's SME Strategy is broadly aligned with this legal framework, particularly through its objective of "ensuring further education, especially in areas of key skills". In particular, the recommendations of the EU Council have been implemented in the national context through a series of concrete measures (e.g., training e-shop and increased offer of micro-credentials) that have been discussed earlier in this chapter.

Nonetheless, a few measures could still be implemented to further align Czech policies with EU guidelines on skills development. For example, the European Skills Agenda emphasises the importance of creating entrepreneurial skills hubs. However, despite a growing incubation and acceleration ecosystem, entrepreneurship education in higher education remains limited. In addition, Czechia could further strengthen policies to support skills development for the green transition, in line with the European Skills Agenda and the European Green Deal.

Conclusions and policy recommendations

Czechia's SME Support Strategy identifies vocational education and training as a strategic priority. Accordingly, skills development programmes have been introduced under the National Recovery Plan, the Operational Programme Employment Plus (OPE +), and the Operational Programme Technology and Application for Competitiveness (OP TAC). While a few of these initiatives specifically target SMEs, such as the OPE+ call to improve business competences within SMEs, most are aimed at upskilling the workforce in general.

Although there has been a strong uptake of some of these programmes – e.g., the e-shop launched by the Ministry of Labour and Social Affairs has attracted over 18 000 users in its first months of operation – further efforts are required to boost participation in training, notably through more readily available information on the types of training, funding mechanisms, and programme conditions. In addition, the scope of training topics could be broadened to include more courses on entrepreneurship skills and green skills. In the area of entrepreneurship education, some promising initiatives have become to emerge, but the offer of entrepreneurship education could become more systemic.

Specific policy recommendations to strengthen workforce skills in Czech SMEs will include:

- Increasing awareness among employers of the system of recognition of prior learning (learning acquired through professional experience or in a non-academic environment), which has been in place in Czechia since 2006, as an important channel to reduce skills mismatches at the firm level and in the wider labour market.
- Enhancing the provision of entrepreneurship education, for example by promoting it further in higher education institutions where there is already an incubator or, more ambitiously, by launching a national entrepreneurship education programme involving the development of a national curriculum.

- Expanding the provision of micro-credentials, especially in areas such as green and digital skills where demand from employers evolves rapidly.

References

Atomico, Google for Start-ups (2022), *Central and Eastern European Start-ups*, https://dealroom.co/uploaded/2022/11/Dealroom-GoogleAtomicCredo-CEE-2022.pdf?x30228. [16]

Bacigalupo, M. et al. (2016), *EntreComp: The Entrepreneurship Competence Framework*, Luxembourg (Luxembourg): Publications Office of the European Union, https://doi.org/10.2791/593884. [18]

Borgonovi, F. et al. (2023), "Emerging trends in AI skill demand across 14 OECD countries", *OECD Artificial Intelligence Papers*, No. 2, OECD Publishing, Paris, https://doi.org/10.1787/7c691b9a-en. [6]

Cathles, A. and J. Navarro (2019), *Disrupting Talent: The Emergence of Coding Bootcamps and the Future of Digital Skills*, Inter-American Development Bank, https://doi.org/10.18235/0001651. [14]

Cedefop (2023), *Skills forecast Czechia*, https://www.cedefop.europa.eu/files/skills_forecast_2023_czechia.pdf. [9]

Chamber of Commerce of Czechia (2024), *Strategic Priorities for the Czech Economy*, https://www.komora.cz/app/uploads/2024/06/brozura_ceskonakrizovatce.pdf. [11]

Council of the European Union (2022), *Council Recommendation of 16 June 2022 on a European approach to micro-credentials for lifelong learning and employability*, https://eur-lex.europa.eu/legal-content/EN/TXT/PDF/?uri=CELEX:32022H0627(02). [23]

Council of the European Union (2022), *Council Recommendation of 16 June 2022 on individual learning accounts (2022/C 243/03)*, https://eur-lex.europa.eu/legal-content/EN/TXT/PDF/?uri=CELEX:32022H0627(03). [24]

European Commission (2020), *Communication from the Commission to the European Parliament, the Council, the European Economic and Social Committee and the Committee of the Regions, COM(2020) 103*, https://eur-lex.europa.eu/legal-content/EN/TXT/?uri=CELEX:52020DC0103. [22]

Eurostat (2023), *Digitalisation in Europe – 2023 edition*, https://ec.europa.eu/eurostat/fr/web/interactive-publications/digitalisation-2023. [7]

Keiretsu Forum (2020), *Start-up Report 2019-2020*, https://media.wix.com/ugd/c955a9_382f291fffe642c689506b1d6b694449.pdf. [15]

Klofsten, M., D. Jones-Evans and L. Pereira (2020), "Teaching science and technology PhD students in entrepreneurship-potential learning opportunities and outcomes", *The Journal of Technology Transfer*, Vol. 46/2, pp. 319-334, https://doi.org/10.1007/s10961-020-09784-8. [19]

Lane, M., M. Williams and S. Broecke (2023), "The impact of AI on the workplace: Main findings from the OECD AI surveys of employers and workers", *OECD Social, Employment and Migration Working Papers*, No. 288, OECD Publishing, Paris, https://doi.org/10.1787/ea0a0fe1-en. [2]

Meghnagi, M. and M. Tuccio (2022), "The recognition of prior learning: Validating general competences", *OECD Social, Employment and Migration Working Papers*, No. 270, OECD Publishing, Paris, https://doi.org/10.1787/2d9fb06a-en. [12]

Ministry of Industry and Trade of Czechia (2022), *Annual Implementation Report of the SME Strategy 2021-2027*, https://www.komora.cz/app/uploads/2024/04/225_23_material.pdf. [5]

OECD (2024), *OECD Employment Outlook 2024: The Net-Zero Transition and the Labour Market*, OECD Publishing, Paris, https://doi.org/10.1787/ac8b3538-en. [1]

OECD (2024), *OECD Going Digital Toolkit*, https://goingdigital.oecd.org/en/indicator/43. [8]

OECD (2023), *Education at a Glance 2023: OECD Indicators*, OECD Publishing, Paris, https://doi.org/10.1787/e13bef63-en. [10]

OECD (2023), "The geography of higher education of Newfoundland and Labrador, Canada: Assessing the role of Memorial University within its regional innovation ecosystem", *OECD SME and Entrepreneurship Papers*, No. 39, OECD Publishing, Paris, https://doi.org/10.1787/5599133d-en. [21]

OECD (2019), *Getting Skills Right: Future-Ready Adult Learning Systems*, Getting Skills Right, OECD Publishing, Paris, https://doi.org/10.1787/9789264311756-en. [4]

OECD/IDB (2022), *Innovative and Entrepreneurial Universities in Latin America*, OECD Skills Studies, OECD Publishing, Paris, https://doi.org/10.1787/ca45d22a-en. [20]

Samek, R. (2022), *Methodology for the Development of Innovation Infrastructures in the Czech Republic*, https://mpo.gov.cz/assets/cz/podnikani/ris3-strategie/projekty-na-podporu-ris3/operacni-program-vyzkum-vyvoj-a-vzdelavani/2023/2/Metodika-rozvoje-inovacnich-infrastruktur-v-CR.pdf. [17]

Varadarajan, S., J. Koh and B. Daniel (2023), "A systematic review of the opportunities and challenges of micro-credentials for multiple stakeholders: learners, employers, higher education institutions and government", *International Journal of Educational Technology in Higher Education*, Vol. 20/1, https://doi.org/10.1186/s41239-023-00381-x. [13]

World Economic Forum (2023), *The Future of Jobs Report 2023*, https://www3.weforum.org/docs/WEF_Future_of_Jobs_2023.pdf. [3]

Notes

[1] Robot intensity is defined as the share of the value of industrial robot stocks over manufacturing value added.

[2] See more data at: "Main skills targeted by CVT courses by type of skill and size class - % of enterprises providing CVT courses", https://ec.europa.eu/eurostat/databrowser/view/trng_cvt_29s__custom_12409997/bookmark/table?lang=en&bookmarkId=991dade6-38ff-4cec-a271-f234c33b8119&c=1722423042116.

[3] Further information on the Amendment to the Employment Law can be found here: https://www.havelpartners.com/amendment-to-the-labour-code-all-that-you-need-to-know-in-a-nutshell/ & http://www.czechcompete.cz/good-governance/legal-reform-and-transparency/amendment-to-the-employment-act-overview-of-new-provisions-applicable-from-july-2024

[4] Further information at: https://www.mpsv.cz/web/cz/jsem-v-kurzu

[5] The main player in this area is the Ministry of Regional Development. Further information at: https://irop.gov.cz/getmedia/79d931b4-d997-4ce4-a810-994a97296bff/IROP_Summary-for-the-Public2020.pdf.aspx?ext=.pdf

[6] A similar initiative was also funded through the Operational Programme "Entrepreneurship and Innovation for Competitiveness" (OP EIC), which was the antecedent of the OP TAC of the Ministry of Industry and Trade, covering the programming period 2014-2020.

[7] For further information on micro-credentials, see: https://www.unesco.org/en/articles/micro-credentials-important-part-bigger-ecosystem

[8] In this report, a start-up is defined as a "company that offers unique, scalable solutions, ideally transforming people's lives." Given the broad nature of this definition, many businesses could potentially fit within it. To address this ambiguity, the authors of the report surveyed entrepreneurs, asking whether they considered their enterprise a start-up. They also delved into the reasons behind their choice of this label over alternative descriptions such as "tradesperson" or "entrepreneur."

5 SME R&D and innovation

Czechia's overall innovation performance is close to the EU average. However, Czech companies, and especially SMEs, spend relatively little on R&D compared to the EU average. Czechia has an integrated innovation strategy that has become more coherent over time, and public spending on R&D has increased between 2017 and 2024. Public support for R&D takes mostly the form of direct support, but programmes tend to be fragmented, which can increase administrative costs. Further improving co-ordination among funding institutions and streamlining programmes could make it easier for SMEs to identify funding opportunities. Improving indirect support for R&D through clearer and more accessible tax incentives, or a possible shift toward payroll-based R&D tax credits, could stimulate greater private investment. More incentives for technology transfer, such as sustained support for technology transfer offices and applied PhD programmes, could strengthen linkages between research and industry. Finally, more capacity-building services for SMEs, which could be delivered through regional innovation centres, could help bolster Czech SME's innovation capabilities.

Key messages

- **Czechia has an average innovation performance at the EU level, although its SMEs tend to spend little on R&D**. In 2023, the country ranked in the 14th position in the European Commission's Innovation Scoreboard, better than other Central and Eastern European (CEE) countries such as Poland, Slovakia, and Hungary. Nonetheless, Czech firms spend relatively little on R&D compared to the EU average, and SMEs are responsible for only a quarter of the overall R&D spending.
- **Czechia benefits from an integrated innovation strategy which informs most of its R&D and innovation (RDI) spending.** Most of Czechia's public spending on RDI is in line with the main priorities of its Smart Specialisation Strategy, with a trend towards more strategic coherence by all relevant public institutions.
- **Czechia's public spending on RDI has increased, but programmes tend to be fragmented and could benefit from further streamlining**. External R&D funding, mostly from European sources, has increased from 0.44% of GDP in 2017 to 0.61% in 2021, while internal public funding hovered around 0.6% of GDP. Public programmes are spread across various initiatives based on their funding sources, which can increase administrative costs and create confusion for SMEs in selecting the most appropriate programme. Streamlining the existing programme offering would facilitate access for SMEs.
- **Czechia could also further encourage private investment in RDI through tax incentives.** Existing tax incentives come with a high degree of uncertainty on whether the applicant will be able to receive the expected tax relief and are more attractive to profitable and larger firms. Clearer allocation rules could encourage a bigger take-up of R&D tax credits. Furthermore, a shift towards a system based on a payroll tax credit, rather than a decrease in corporate profit taxation, could further encourage innovation by decreasing the cost of R&D spending directly in the year when this takes place and by making the use of the tax benefit simpler.
- **Czechia could also encourage more proactively the transfer of technology between universities and businesses.** At present, Czech faculty members have limited incentives to collaborate with businesses, as most of their funding is related to teaching and academic research. Czechia could provide longer-term funding to the Technology Transfer Offices (TTO) of universities, as a means to encourage business-research collaborations. Alternatively, it could modify the existing funding structure so that such collaborations increase universities' resources. Finally, it could create a pilot applied PhD programme.
- **Capacity building also has a role to play in strengthening the innovation capabilities of SMEs**. This includes not only consulting regarding the various available funding opportunities, but also mentorship schemes, business consulting services and incubation programmes. Regional innovation centres such as the JIC (Brno, South Moravia) could be well placed to offer these services.

SME performance in R&D and innovation

Czechia has an average innovation performance among EU countries

Czechia has an average innovation performance compared to other EU countries. Based on the 2023 edition of the European Commission's European Innovation Scoreboard, Czechia is a moderate innovator, ranking in the 14th position in the EU, though above other Central and Eastern European (CEE) countries like Poland, Slovakia, and Hungary. Innovation gathers mostly around large cities, which act as innovation centres. The capital region of Prague is the only one in the country that qualifies as an innovation leader at the European level, followed by the Brno region (Jihovýchod), which qualifies as a strong innovator (European Commission, 2023[1]). This is not surprising, as both cities host the main universities and research centres of Czechia. All other Czech regions score as either moderate or emerging innovators in the EU context.

Some of this moderate innovation performance can be explained by low total R&D spending. Despite an increase in public funding in recent years, Czechia's R&D spending is still below the EU average: 2% of GDP in 2021, up from 1.77% in 2017, but still below the EU average of 2.15%.

While government funding of R&D has recently increased, business funding as a share of GDP has remained stable, standing at about 60% of the EU average in 2021 (Figure 5.1). This is also visible from other statistics. For example, Czechia had no company in the top 2 500 industrial R&D spenders, according to the 2022 EU Industrial R&D Investment Scoreboard (Grassano et al., 2022[2]).[1]

Figure 5.1. Gross Expenditure on R&D (GERD) by source of funding, Czechia and selected countries, 2021 and 2017

Percentage of GDP

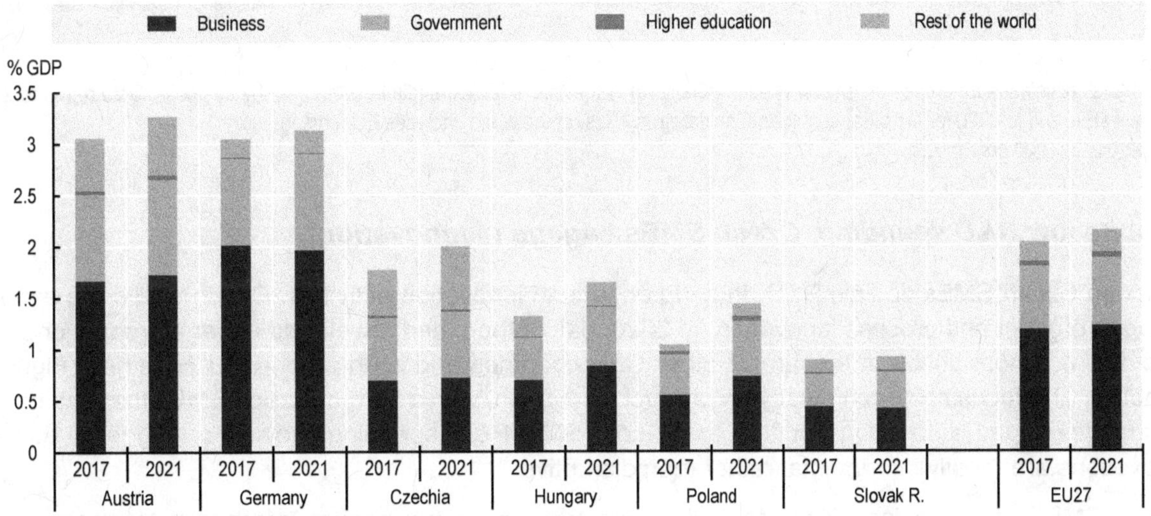

Note: The category "Rest of the world" includes European funds.
Source: OECD R&D Statistics database.

Czech SMEs are small players in formal R&D

Against the backdrop of limited national R&D spending, SMEs are even smaller players. In 2020, they accounted for a quarter (27%) of total business enterprise R&D (BERD) spending, corresponding to 0.3% of GDP, which is less than Austria or Hungary (respectively, 0.66% and 0.48%) (Figure 5.2). It follows that most business R&D in Czechia is performed by large companies, which are more likely to take the risks associated with innovation thanks to larger internal resources.

Figure 5.2. Business enterprise R&D (BERD) expenditure by funding sector and firm size, Czechia and selected countries, 2020

Percentage values

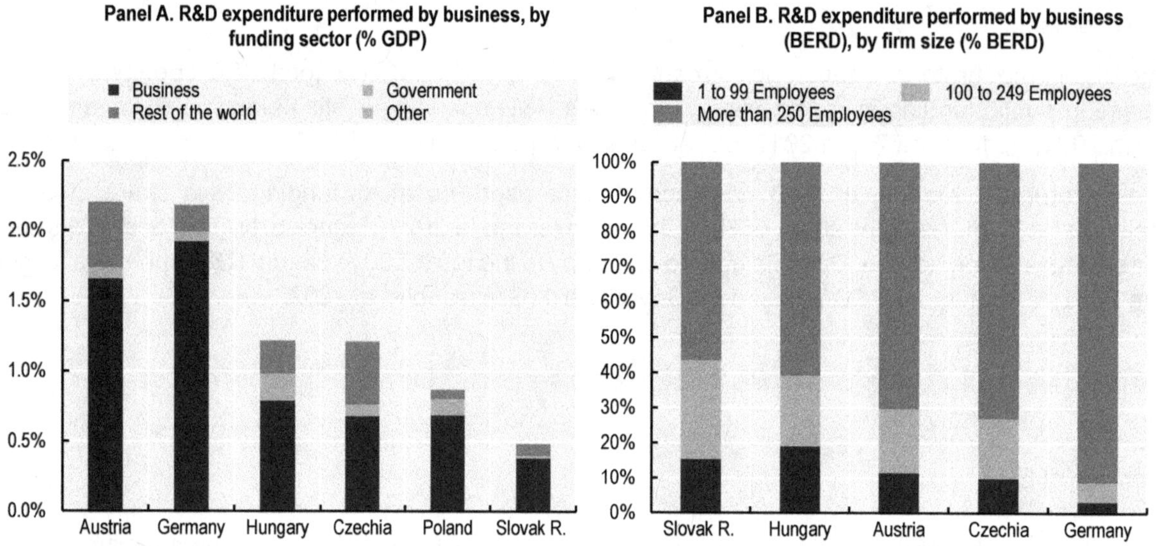

Note: BERD (Business Enterprise Intramural R&D Expenditure) is the total R&D expenditure performed by business. Data refers to 2019 for AUT and DEU and to 2020 for the other countries. The category "Rest of the world" includes EU funding.
Source: OECD R&D database.

Despite low R&D spending, Czech SMEs engage in innovation

Although Czech SMEs do little R&D, they do engage in innovation activities. Czech SMEs are especially active in product and process innovation: in 2020, half of them had developed either a product or process innovation, almost double the share of other CEE countries and sixth among EU countries (Figure 5.3, Panel A). The focus has been mostly on product innovation, with a third of Czech SMEs that had declared having developed innovations in this area. Low SME R&D spending, however, suggests that SME innovations are mostly incremental rather than disruptive.

Czech SMEs are also less likely to collaborate with other businesses compared to peer countries (Figure 5.3, Panel B). Collaboration is crucial for innovation. In 2020, the share of innovative companies which declared they collaborated with other businesses was 30% for small companies and 45% for medium companies. For non-innovative companies, by contrast, it was only 5%. Stronger co-operation between SMEs and other members of the national innovation system (e.g. larger companies and research centres) could improve innovation performance through enhanced access to new ideas, talent, and technologies (OECD, 2023[3]).

Figure 5.3. SME innovation performance, Czechia and selected countries, 2020

Percentage of firms

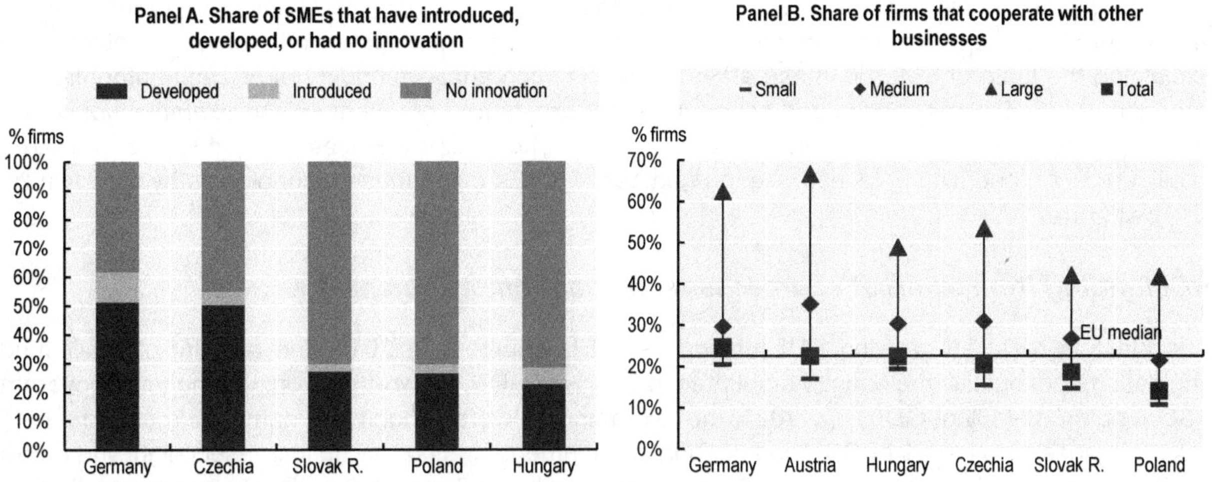

Note: In Panel A, the category "Developed" includes three categories in the Community Innovation Survey: 1) enterprises that have developed product innovation themselves, with market novelties (profile I), 2) enterprises that developed product innovations themselves without market novelties (profile II), and 3) enterprises that have developed business process innovations themselves, without product innovation (profile III). Category "Introduced" refers to enterprises that have introduced but not themselves developed innovations (profile IV). Category "No innovation" includes three profiles: a) Enterprises that have (ongoing or abandoned) innovation activities but not introduced any innovation (profile V), b) enterprises that have no innovation activities but potential to innovate (profile VI), and c) Enterprises that have no innovation activities and no potential to innovate (profile VII). In Panel B, the horizontal bar in Panel B refers to the median EU country, all firms.
Source: Eurostat Community Innovation Survey 2020 (https://ec.europa.eu/eurostat/web/science-technologyinnovation/data/database). The calculations in Panel B come from OECD SME and Entrepreneurship Outlook 2023 (OECD, 2023[3]).

SME R&D and innovation policies: Mid-term evaluation of the national SME Strategy

Czechia has an integrated national innovation strategy

Czechia has an integrated national innovation strategy that defines clear priorities for public investment. The National Research and Innovation Strategy for Smart Specialisation (i.e., RIS3 Strategy) singles out the main technologies, known as key enabling technologies (i.e., KETs), and the main sectors, known as specialisation domains, to be prioritised for public funding.[2] These technologies and sectors are prioritised across multiple national strategies and programmes.

For example, CzechInvest, the national investment agency, has changed its strategy to make it more aligned with these priorities. The agency has developed a technology incubation programme that offers mentoring and public support of up to EUR 200 000 per company for the development of proofs of concept in one of the seven priority areas identified by the RIS3 Strategy. It has also set up sectoral hubs for each priority area, which act as centres bringing together firms with R&D capabilities, start-ups, and public programmes.

Czechia has also developed a network of regional innovation centres. One of the most known examples is JIC-Brno, the regional innovation centre of South Moravia, which was also one of the first to align with the RIS3 strategy (OECD, 2024[4]). JIC was established in 2003 as an association between universities and subnational governments and has become an important pillar of the regional innovation ecosystem, offering a wide range of programmes across all business innovation phases (e.g., workshops for mature companies, business mentoring and networking for scale-ups, and an accelerator programme for start-ups).

Going forward, to further better align with the RIS3 Strategy, Czechia's SME Strategy could become more specific on its innovation priorities. Notably, the SME Strategy mentions supporting innovative entrepreneurship and business innovation in key enabling technologies and priority sectors, without explaining the state of SMEs in these areas, whereas such analysis could help Czech authorities better understand the current baseline and set appropriate targets for improvement. An example would involve understanding the position of SMEs in the use of technologies such as biotechnology and Artificial Intelligence (AI) and aiming to increase the number of SMEs using these technologies by a certain target or growth rate.

RDI funding from external sources is significant but fragmented

Czechia has received growing RDI funding from EU sources. In 2017, the amount of R&D funding originating from outside the country amounted to 0.44% of GDP, or two-thirds of the amount of government R&D funding (0.61% of GDP). By 2021, the two amounts were roughly the same, with external funding having increased to 0.61% of GDP and national government funding having increased slightly to 0.65% of GDP. External funding mostly includes EU sources such as Horizon 2020 or the Recovery and Resilience Facility (RRF), as well as some R&D funded by foreign companies, such as branches of MNEs that are active in Czechia (OECD, 2015[5]).

Some of the effects of this increased funding are already visible. Between 2021 and 2023, Czechia showed the strongest progression in the European Innovation Scoreboard. In 2021, its score was one-fifth below the EU average score (89 compared to 106). By 2023, Czechia's score was 103, only 5% below the EU average of 108. The strongest improvements were in the categories of SMEs introducing process and product innovations, employment in innovative enterprises, number of innovators, and venture capital expenditures.

One downside of EU funding, however, is that in the context of Czechia it is implemented in a highly fragmented way (see Box 5.1 for an overview of the main EU funding programmes supporting RDI in Czechia). This makes it difficult for companies to keep track of funding opportunities and programme requirements and facilitates the emergence of companies that become skilled at the administrative processes involved in securing EU funding. Moreover, fragmentation implies high administrative costs both for SMEs, which must track opportunities and submit multiple applications, and the public administration, which must oversee and manage several programmes and calls at the same time.

Box 5.1. Main EU funding sources for RDI by SMEs in Czechia

The Recovery and Resilience Plan (RRP) is a large-scale funding programme initiated by the European Union in the wake of the Covid-19 pandemic. Of the EUR 8.4 billion (3% of GDP) allocated to Czechia's RRP, RDI expenditures amounted to 7%, two percentage points below the EU average (European Commission, 2024[6]). Many RRP programmes are targeted towards SME and midcap support, especially in areas identified by the RIS3 strategy:

- A programme to fund the digitalisation of nearly 400 enterprises, of which at least two-thirds should be SMEs and mid-caps, with a focus on process innovation through digitalisation.
- A call to fund 90 SMEs to implement individual innovation projects (either process, product, or organisation), as well as a call to create National Centres of Competence and encourage at least 60 SMEs to co-operate in RDI projects with a public research organisation.

- A budget of EUR 200 million for public R&D consortia in priority medical sciences and related social sciences, which should be awarded by public tenders.

The OP TAC (Operational Programme Technology and Application for Competitiveness) is an Operational Programme funded by the ERDF (European Regional Development Fund), which aims to encourage economic, social and territorial cohesion across the EU. The OP TAC has a budget allocation of EUR 3 billion, which covers several innovation programmes with a focus on SMEs, especially for knowledge transfer and digital enterprises. Given OP TAC's focus on territorial cohesion, calls are not available for firms from the Prague region, which has too high an income.

The OP JT (Operational Programme Just Transition) (budget EUR 1.6 billion) is an Operational Programme funded by the Just Transition Fund, which aims to support the regions most affected by the transition to climate neutrality. Czechia's OP JT focuses on the development of the three coal regions of Czechia (Karlovy Vary, Moravia-Silesia and Ústí), and has RDI and SMEs as declared priorities.

A smaller programme called Digital Europe funds digitalisation projects for businesses, separate from other funding sources. For instance, some of Czechia's European Digital Innovation Hubs (EDIHs), such as the Cybersecurity Hub, are funded in part by the RRP and in part by the Digital Europe Programme. Most of these programmes cover the current EU budget cycle (2021-2027), with some expenditures being eligible until 2029.

Going forward, Czech SMEs would benefit from a more streamlined approach to RDI public support. Notably, a smaller number of larger programmes disbursing bigger sums would limit administrative costs while ensuring that high-quality projects receive the funding they need to progress. Stronger co-ordination between the various sources of funding would also be needed to ensure that programme objectives do not overlap, and that firms have a better understanding of which programmes are best suited for them. Funding tickets could be split according to different stages of business development, with clear pathways from one stage to the other. This would not mean that only large-scale projects are funded, but that firms can see a clear progression if they meet specific development milestones. This would avoid the so-called "valley-of-death", where intermediary steps in the innovation process are deprived of funding and firms cannot reach the final stage of commercialisation

Some Czech institutions are already going in this direction. For instance, Czechia's Technology Agency has combined multiple funding programmes into the SIGMA programme, an eight-year programme supporting applied research projects between 2022 and 2029 (see Box 5.2) (Ministry of Industry and Trade, 2024[7]).

Box 5.2. The SIGMA programme of Czechia's Technology Agency (TA CR)

SIGMA is a programme that supports applied research and innovation and is managed by Czechia's Technology Agency (TA CR). Its current design covers eight years, from 2022 to 2029. It is a complex programme that includes several sub-objectives, some of which have been consolidated from previous programmes of the same agency (e.g. GAMA, DELTA, ETA, ZETA):

- Sub-objective 1. *Activities of so-called pre-application research*, which aim to speed up innovation and make it easier to transfer knowledge and results from research organisations into the business world. This includes ensuring stable technology transfer offices in research organisations.
- Sub-objective 2. *Early-stage researchers and equality of opportunities in applied research projects,* consisting of activities which aim to encourage early-stage research and incentives to

- be involved in applied research projects, with a focus of ensuring equal opportunities across genders.
- Sub-objective 3. *Support of the innovation potential of social sciences, humanities and arts,* which aims to increase the innovative potential of these domains and apply the resulting outputs to new products, processes and services.
- Sub-objective 4. *International collaboration*, which aims to encourage international collaboration and position Czechia as a destination for cutting-edge research. Projects in this area can also complement other funding sources, such as the EU Operational Programmes.
- Sub-objective 5. *Cross-sectional support*, including activities that strengthen the overall RDI environment in Czechia but are not currently covered by other programmes. Examples include the development of regional innovation ecosystems, support for multidisciplinary approaches in innovation projects, and support for current R&D needs.

Aid intensity varies across sub-objectives and projects, ranging between 75% and 100%. At the end of 2023, the planned expenditure of the programme was CZK 9 billion, of which three quarters was from the state budget.

Source: Technology Agency of the Czech Republic (2024[8]). *Programme to Support Applied Research and Innovation SIGMA.*

Multi-stage innovation vouchers could boost business patenting

Despite an increase in the past years, patenting levels remain relatively low. In 2021, Czechia had 31 patent applications per million inhabitants, a 50% increase from 2017 but still less than a third of the EU average (Figure 5.4). Czechia was also towards the bottom of the patenting ranking among OECD countries, ranking in the 25th position out of 38 countries in 2021.

Figure 5.4. Patent applications in Czechia and selected countries, 2021

Patent applications per million inhabitants in 2021

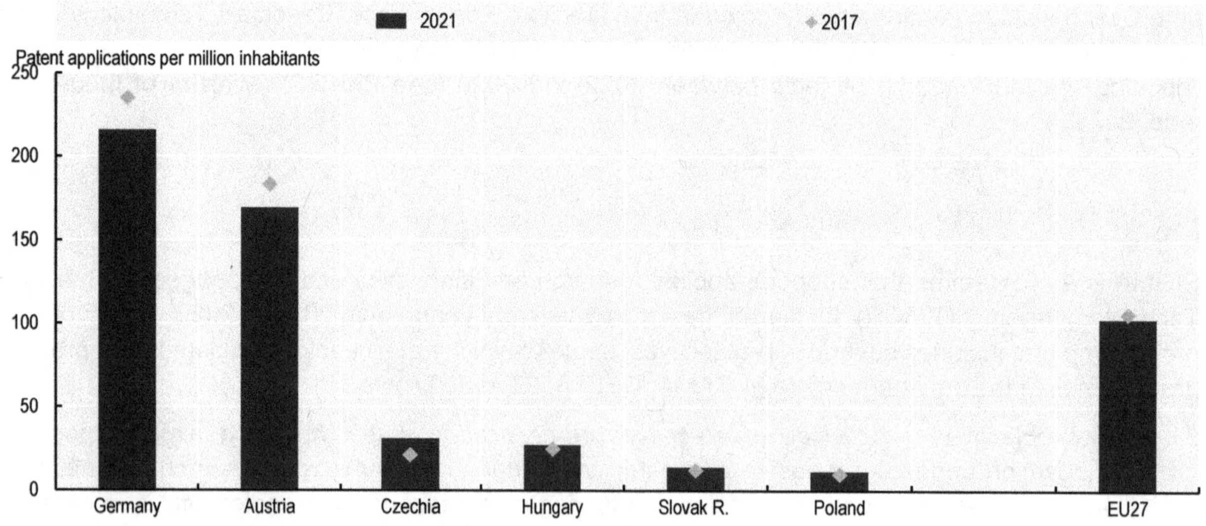

Source: OECD Main Science and Technology Indicators (MSTI database) and OECD Population data.

SMEs seeking support for patenting their innovations can benefit from two innovation voucher schemes running in parallel. The first, which is funded by the SME Fund and managed by the EU Intellectual Property Organisation (EUIPO), offers up to EUR 3 500 to SMEs which register a patent. The second one, funded by OP TAC, is broader and covers multiple intellectual property (IP) services, with a minimum of CZK 50 000 and a maximum of CZK 500 000 per voucher.[3]

The two voucher schemes could be combined into a multi-stage voucher scheme, which would support SMEs throughout the entire IP protection process, from the prospecting phase to the patenting phase. Firms that are accepted and successfully complete the first phases could be fast-tracked into the next phase. This would provide SMEs with funding certainty as well as incentives to complete the IP protection process, possibly increasing patenting rates.

The current national R&D tax credit policy has low and declining take-up

Czechia's tax system includes indirect incentives for R&D, in the form of a tax allowance on the corporate income tax for private R&D spending. This allows firms to deduct 100% of R&D expenses that are below the expenses of the previous tax year, with a 10% extra deduction for expenses above those of the previous year to further reward incremental R&D spending. R&D expenses financed through public funds are excluded to avoid double public funding. In 2014, the Czech tax credit system broadened its coverage of eligible R&D costs to include external R&D services provided by public research institutions, such as universities and other knowledge-based organisations. Czechia's implicit subsidy rate[4] is in line with the OECD average for loss-making SMEs (around 15%) and slightly higher for profit-making SMEs (21% in Czechia and 18% for the OECD average – see Figure 5.5, Panel A).

Despite having implicit subsidy rates in line with the OECD, Czech firms have a limited take-up of tax incentives for R&D. According to the OECD R&D Tax Incentives database, in 2023, R&D tax incentives amounted to less than 0.05% of GDP, three times less than the OECD average (Figure 5.5, Panel B). The number of companies receiving the tax benefit has also decreased in recent years, from 1 300 in 2015 to 750 in 2022 (Czech Statistical Office, 2024[9]).

Figure 5.5. Implicit tax subsidy rates for R&D and total government incentives for R&D, Czechia and selected countries, 2021 and 2023

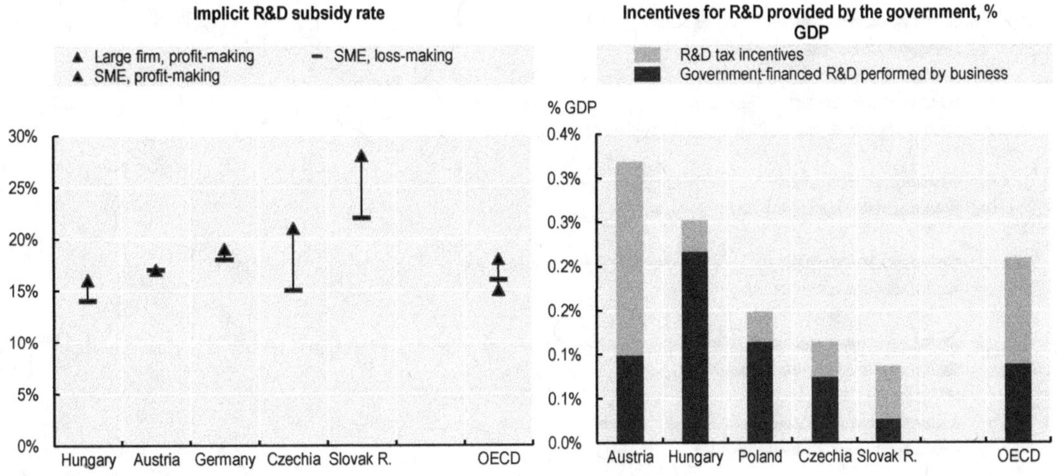

Note: The implicit tax subsidy rate on R&D expenditures is calculated as 1 minus the B-index, i.e. before-tax income needed by a representative firm to break even on one additional monetary unit of R&D. Data in Panel A refer to the year 2021, data in Panel B refer to 2023.
Source: Data for the graph in Panel A comes from the OECD R&D database. The data for the graph in Panel B comes from the OECD R&D Tax Incentives database.

Several design factors may help explain this low take-up. First, tax allowances are only useful if firms have a positive taxable profit. However, many firms, especially start-ups, invest from external sources and do not turn a profit until years later. For firms which do not have significant profits, a tax allowance on corporate income tax does not alleviate liquidity problems.

Second, existing carry-forward provisions further limit the capacity of this policy to alleviate liquidity constraints. Expenses can be deducted within three years from when they have occurred, a time limit that is quite strict compared to the experience of other OECD countries. Tax benefits which have not been used within three years are, therefore, lost. However, many innovations require a longer period to pay off, which means many R&D spenders may not benefit from the Czech tax allowance as it is currently designed.

Third, there is a requirement that the investment be used for innovation, which is hard to define by tax authorities. The result is that a large share of requests for the allowance is rejected, increasing uncertainty and limiting the effectiveness of the incentive.

As a result of these design issues, few firms have recently had access to the R&D tax credit. The number of SMEs that received the R&D tax credit halved, from 1 000 in 2015 to close to 550 in 2022. The number of large firms also decreased but at a lower rate, dropping by one-third in the same period. As a result, the share of R&D tax incentives going to SMEs decreased from 33% in 2015 to 20% in 2022 (Figure 5.6).

In addition to policy design factors, it should also be considered that the presence of many innovation grants, mostly funded by EU sources (see above), may have decreased over time the attractiveness of the national R&D tax credit policy for Czech companies. However, EU funding is expected to decrease in coming years, as Czechia's average income per capita gets closer and closer to the EU average, pointing to the importance of improving the national R&D tax policy design to ensure that local SMEs continue to benefit from innovation funding.

Figure 5.6. Share of R&D tax budget by firm size, CZK million and number of companies, 2015-2022

Amount of R&D tax incentives going to firms (CZK million, upper bar) and the number of firms getting the incentive (lower bar)

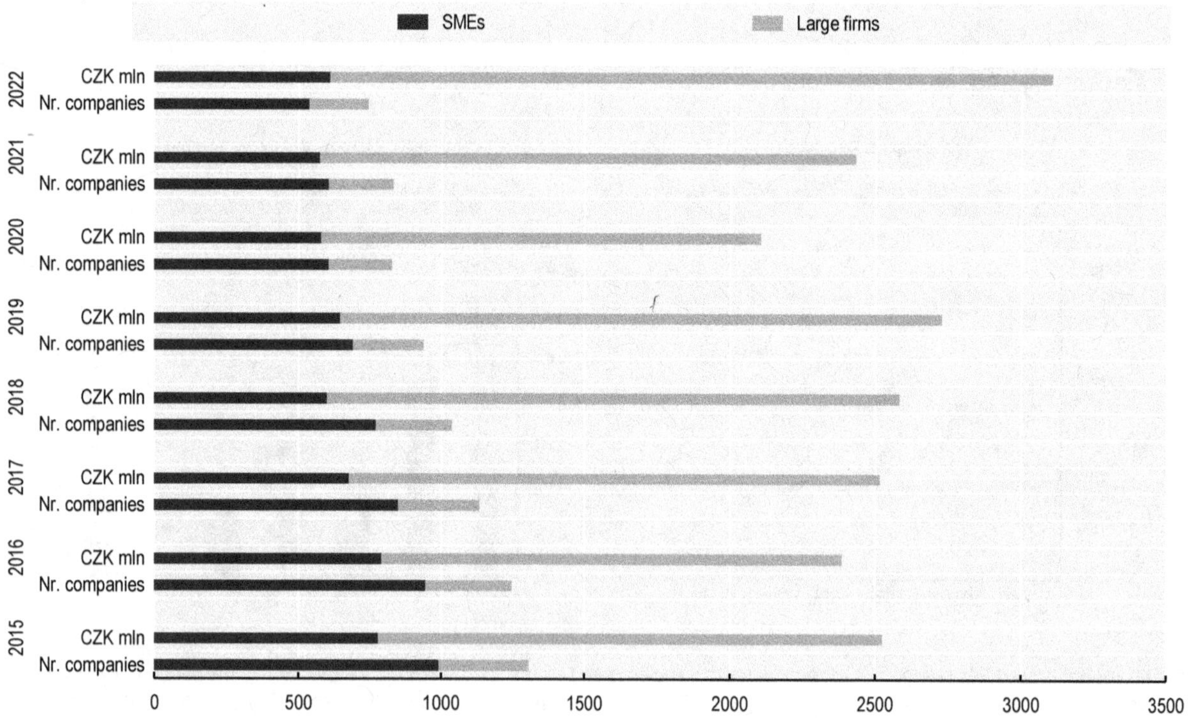

Source: Czech Statistical Institute

Selected reforms could increase the attractiveness of the national R&D tax credit scheme

Against this backdrop, three policy options could be considered to reform the national R&D tax credit system and make it more appealing to local SMEs.

First, the tax authority, which is the government entity in charge with the implementation of the R&D tax credit, could increase take-up by being more lenient in the application of existing requirements. One strategy would be to accept more types of evidence that expenses are truly used for R&D[5]; a clear list of eligible costs could be provided, together with a list of accepted proofs, to clarify conditions for SMEs. Another strategy would be for the tax authority to partner with other public institutions, such as the technology agency, to evaluate applications, as was done in a pilot project in 2023. The technology agency should have better understanding of whether a firm's R&D project is truly innovative, whereas the limited technical expertise of the tax authority may lead to an overly cautious assessment.

Second, carry-forward provisions could be extended from the current three years to five-ten years, with a view to increasing investment returns from R&D. In particular, radical innovation projects, which tend to take longer to show returns, would become more attractive if firms could use their acquired tax deductions over a longer period of time.

Third, the base of the tax incentive could change, which would be the most radical reform of the three options. In particular, the deduction from the corporate income tax could be replaced with a credit on the labour costs associated with R&D staff, similar to the system in place in the Netherlands. Most firms that perform R&D have to employ dedicated personnel and thus pay R&D-related labour costs. Since in this case the tax credit would apply in the same year of the R&D expenditure, this reform would mitigate the liquidity issues associated with the current R&D tax credit policy.

These three reforms could be implemented on a stand-alone basis, although they would have the largest impact on R&D spending if they were introduced together.

There should be stronger encouragement of university-industry technology transfer

There is also scope in Czechia for improving the transfer of knowledge and technology from university to industry as a means to further encourage research commercialisation and productivity growth. According to the World Economic Forum (WEF) survey of business executives, Czechia's level of collaboration between industry and university had improved from a level of four in 2020 to close to five in 2023, on a 1-7 scale. This places Czechia ahead of countries such as Austria and Poland and slightly below Germany (Figure 5.7).

Figure 5.7. Survey evidence on collaboration between business and universities, Czechia and selected countries, 2023 and 2020.

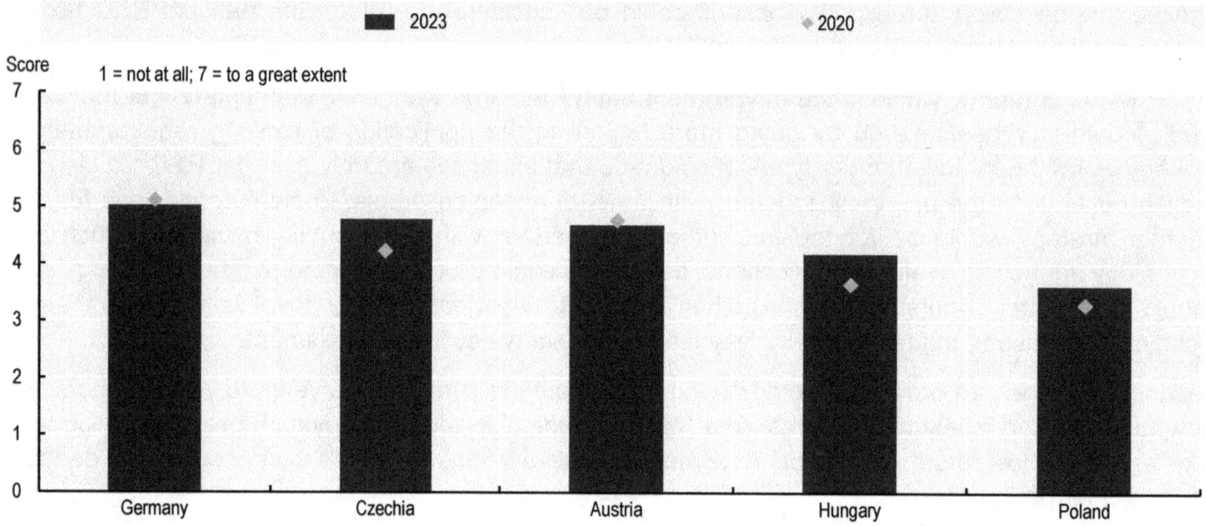

Note. Score based on the following question posed to business executives: In your country, to what extent do business and universities collaborate on research and development?
Source: World Economic Forum Executive Opinion Survey 2023.

Nonetheless, the existing national system of university funding does not give strong incentives for industry-university collaboration[6]. Four-fifths of university funding, at least for the 26 public universities, come from the state budget in the form of institutional funding, which is divided into three portions (Eurydice, 2024[10]): blocked funding, performance-based funding, and social demand funding.

The largest portion, known as blocked (or stability) funding, accounts for 75% of the total and is allocated based on fixed proportions that reflect the size of each university. This allocation remains relatively constant and is not recalculated annually. The second source, performance-based funding, covers 20% of institutional funding and is determined by eight indicators, such as graduation rate, research and development output, and the presence of foreign students, which are evaluated annually. Applied research outputs are, therefore, included in this 20% of university funding which also includes many other things[7]. The final source, social demand funding, comprises 3-5% of the institutional funding and is aimed at addressing societal needs, such as shortages in specific professions (Research, Development and Innovation Council of Czechia, 2024[11]).

More recently, there have been some changes to better encourage industry-university collaboration. The long-term assessment of universities and research institutes, which takes place every five years, now includes measures of societal relevance, such as institutional collaboration with businesses and government institutions. Five different components are considered. The largest component, accounting for 50% of the final score, is the quality and quantity of research, which is evaluated by an international panel. The second most important component, "social relevance", includes applied research, industry-university collaboration, and partnerships with the private sector, and holds a 30% weight on the final score. So far, the focus has primarily been on the existence of such collaborations, but in the future universities are also expected to provide evidence on the effectiveness of these collaborations, for example in terms of university spin-offs (Research, Development and Innovation Council of Czechia, 2024[11]).

Additional reforms to further strengthen university-industry collaboration could include the following ones. First, the national government could empower existing technology transfer offices (TTOs) through targeted, performance-based funding with a longer-term horizon. Most large universities, such as those in Prague and Brno, have some form of technology transfer office that can attract external funds, such as those from OP JAC (Operational Programme Johannes Amos Comenius) or past national technology transfer programmes such as TRIO (Box 5.3). However, these grants do not ensure financial stability, as they are only available for a couple of years and, upon expiration, universities need to compete again in new calls. This financial uncertainty makes it difficult to attract professional talent with the right mix of industry and academic experience. Strengthening TTOs through longer-term funding, conditioned on performance, could provide these offices with more financial certainty and allow them to attract higher-skilled professionals who would be better able to build longer-term relationships between university and industry.

Box 5.3. The TRIO programme evaluation

The TRIO programme was a national programme which supported applied R&D collaborations between businesses and research institutes in Key Enabling Technologies (photonics, micro-and nanoelectronics, nanotechnology, industrial biotechnology, advanced materials and manufacturing technologies) and the co-operation between enterprises and research institutes. It took the form of four public tenders between 2016 and 2018, which attracted almost 1 500 applicants and had an average acceptance rate of 34%. SMEs represented two-thirds of the beneficiaries and aid. By 2022, the programme was expected to have cost CZK 9 billion, with an average aid intensity, i.e. the share of the project covered from public funds, of 68%.

The programme had several advantages. It was aligned with Czechia's innovation and RIS3 strategies and aimed to encourage the transfer of technology between academic research and business, by supporting applied R&D collaborations. It provided higher aid intensity to small companies (45% to 80%, depending on the type of activity, versus 25% to 65% for large companies). Project proposals went through a thorough evaluation, which involved a mix of public servants with knowledge of the various KETs and external experts.

The programme also had some shortcomings. The software that was used for monitoring and administration was bulky, had limited functionalities, and became obsolete to the point that it could only be run on special servers of the Ministry of Industry and Trade, which was administering the programme. The programme was also complex and prone to fund mismanagement. After auditing a third of the projects, around 10% of the audited amount was estimated to be breaching budgetary discipline. The evaluation concluded that most irregularities were caused by "ignorance of the contractual conditions", which may also suggest complex administrative requirements.

The TRIO programme had limited results, although a formal evaluation, which would have included the creation of a control group, was not conducted. As of early 2024, when 192 of the 495 supported projects had been implemented for at least three years, sales had reached 40% of the target. Small and large companies were the furthest away from meeting the respective targets, reaching between 33% and 37% of the target, while medium companies had reached almost double, close to 65% of the original target. Some of this underperformance may have also been caused by the negative global context during the time of programme implementation, which spanned the Covid-19 pandemic and Russia's war against Ukraine.

Source: Ministry of Industry and Trade (2024[12]). *Final Evaluation of the TRIO Programme.*

Second, the national government could better reward applied research at the university level, for example by changing the weights used in the performance-based part of the national university funding system, notably by granting heavier weights to private-public research and technology transfer programmes. In this area, another option would be to create a specific funding programme for TTOs, with funding generous enough to persuade universities to apply for funding. A wage bonus for faculty members who engage in knowledge-transfer activities would be a further option, as done by Spain through the so-called *sexenio de transferencia* (i.e., six-year transfer) (OECD, 2021[13]).

Third, the government could consider the development of applied PhD programmes, also known as professional doctorates. Such programmes are joint ventures between a university and one or several businesses, where a PhD student undergoes rigorous research in the pursuit of solving a practical problem for the business(es). The industry involvement ensures that the problem being treated is of practical value, as the private partner needs to cover part of the salary costs of the PhD student. The involvement of the university, on the other hand, ensures that the research meets the standard of academic quality necessary for a doctorate degree.

Different policies could be considered to enhance research commercialisation

Innovative SMEs often encounter a gap between the support available in the early stages of their research and innovation process and the final step of commercialisation (i.e., the so-called "valley of death"). There is some evidence that Czech firms may be facing such a gap. According to the Czech Statistical Office, around half of Czech firms (most of which are SMEs) had introduced new-to-market product innovations in the period 2020-2022. However, revenues from novel products were only 8% of sales in that period, half compared to the 16% of 2014.[8]

The Czech government could explore different options to bridge the "valley of death" and support the research commercialisation efforts of SMEs. One first option would be to target grants towards SMEs with high-potential R&D projects, for example trough special calls for SMEs wanting to commercialise their innovative technologies in the priority areas identified by the smart specialisation strategy. Czechia is already supporting SMEs to bring innovations to market, through calls under the SIGMA programme of the technology agency (sub-objective 1 – commercialisation) or OP TAC's innovation challenge call, which focused on projects with TRL (technology readiness level) above 5.[9] Supporting SMEs both in the technical innovation process, as OP TAC's call does, and in the business development process, as SIGMA does, can further develop the innovation capabilities of these businesses. These programmes could be better streamlined according to SMEs' needs rather than funding sources, for instance by setting up a larger commercialisation call with different arms – business development, technology development, financing development, etc.

A second policy option to support research commercialisation would be to create demand for innovative goods and services through public procurement[10]. Public procurement for innovation (PPI) programmes enable governments to act as early technology adopters, thus easing research commercialisation. For instance, Innovative Solutions Canada (ISC) is a Canadian PPI programme that aims to encourage innovation among SMEs and is focussed on strategic technologies. The yearly budget of the programme (CAD 150 million, i.e., about EUR 93 million) is ensured by mandating a subset of public sector organisations to contribute 1% of their R&D budget towards the programme. The ISC programme is split according to the TRL level: i) the "Challenge Stream" for early-stage R&D; ii) the "Testing Stream" for later-stage prototype testing; iii) the "Pathway to Commercialisation for SME innovators" stream, for bringing innovations to market.[11] The public procurement service of Canada supports the procurement process for the contracts, the federal innovation department (Innovation, Science, and Economic Development Canada) leads the program delivery, and the National Research Council provides technical and industrial expertise. Czechia could consider developing something similar, involving in the programme the national procurement office, the technology agency and the Ministry of Industry and Trade.

While PPI programmes hold promise, some attention in implementation is needed. Indeed, they require a good understanding of the technology needs and specificities on the side of the government, so that evaluation criteria accurately match the needs of the institution organising the tender, encourage the development of the technology, and allow an objective project evaluation. SMEs may also be discouraged by the large administrative costs required to win a government contract, as the involved documents often require a level of administrative sophistication that most SMEs lack. Finally, such programmes may be costly, as SMEs and start-ups may not be able to develop new technologies as cost-effectively as very large companies.

A third and final policy option for encouraging the commercialisation of innovative products by SMEs would be to set up joint financing schemes between the government and private sector investors. Governments support can take the form of grants, preferential loans, or equity investments. In these schemes, governments typically leave the selection of beneficiaries to private investors, who are better placed to assess the innovative potential of the supported company. Nevertheless, these schemes may still require significant administrative capacity from the government. Private investors need to be chosen carefully, and the programme must be structured in a way that provides investors with promising financial returns and some level of regulatory certainty. Selection criteria also require a careful trade-off. If they are too strict, the programme may not attract enough SMEs or may attract only those that would have also attracted private investors alone, limiting the additionality of the policy. If they are too loose, the programme may end up enticing too many low-quality applications.

One example of joint private-public support programme is Korea's TIPS (Tech Incubator Programme for Start-up). TIPS combines a standard incubation/accelerator programme with private equity investment and a top-up scheme from R&D funds that is only partially repayable, and only in case of success. Firms propose their innovative projects to accelerators that are partners of the TIPS programmes. The accelerators select their preferred candidates and provide them with mentorship and some equity funding, which can be up to twice the investment made by the founders. As the R&D process advances, the government can provide up to KRW 500 million (EUR 500 000) in R&D funding and the accelerator may provide further equity investments, spread across various stages. If the project is successful, firms need to pay up to 10% of the R&D fund back to the government.[12]

Soft forms of innovation support should be better pursued

The Czech government could also consider the introduction of more programmes that build managerial and innovation skills in SMEs. At present, SME innovation programmes mostly focus on grants and subsidies. These programmes tend to have high costs and require a careful selection of participants in order to ensure that public funds are targeted optimally. However, non-financial support could also prompt more SMEs to innovate. In 2021-2022, Czech SMEs were as integrated with higher education institutions as the OECD median country and less likely to adopt digital technologies than the OECD median (Figure 5.8). Programmes that would support digital technology adoption or stronger co-operation with universities could also encourage SMEs to engage in innovation activities, possibly with small administrative costs.

Figure 5.8. SME integration of networks or use of network technologies in Czechia, 2021 and 2022

From 0 (none) to max 200 (OECD median = 100)

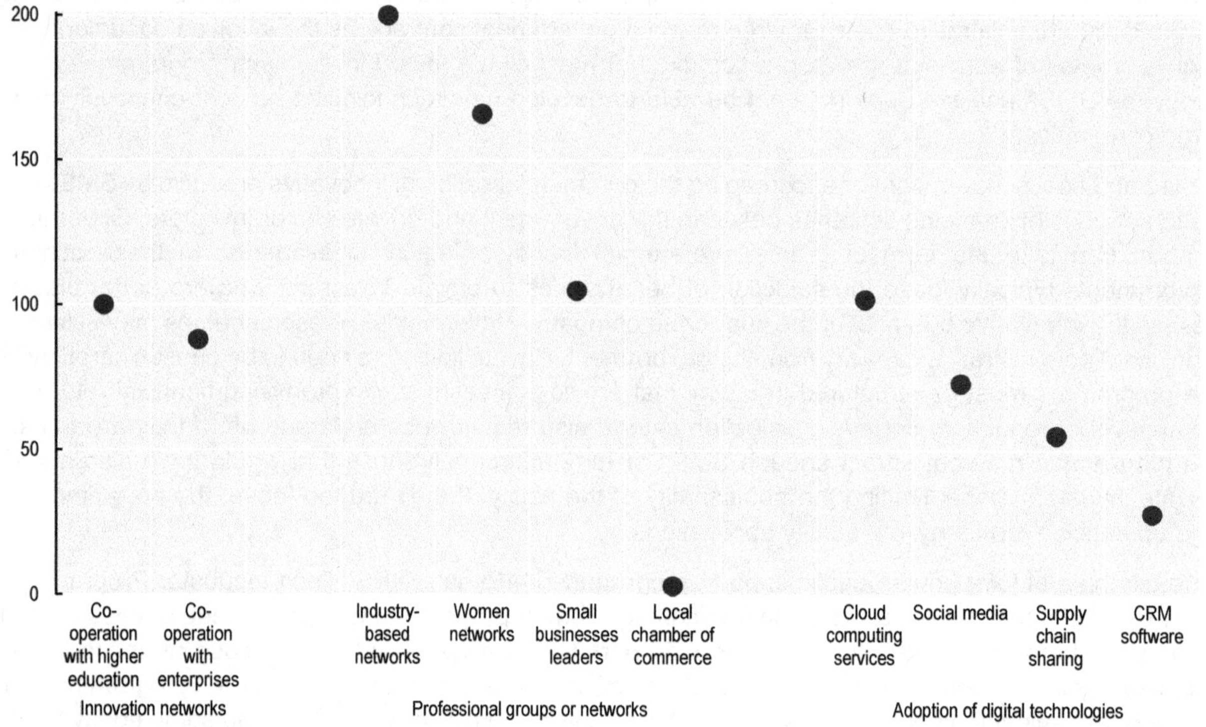

Note: Indicators are presented in the form of benchmarking indices and reported on a common scale from 0 to 200 (0 being the lowest OECD value, 100 the median value, and 200 the highest). Innovation networks include firms co-operating on innovation activities with universities or other higher education institutions; firms co-operating on innovation activities with enterprises engaged in international collaboration; firms co-operating on innovation activities with private business enterprises outside the enterprise group. Only the responses from owners and managers of the business are used in the analysis. Source: Innovation networks: 2021 OECD survey of national Innovation Statistics and Eurostat Community Innovation Survey (OECD, 2021; Eurostat, 2022); Adoption of platform and network technologies: OECD ICT Access and Usage by Businesses; Professional groups: 2022 OECD-World Bank-Meta Future of Business Survey.
Source: OECD SME and Entrepreneurship Outlook 2023 (OECD, 2023[3]).

For example, regional innovation centres could help link local SMEs with possible financiers, suppliers, or clients. Such centres could also be a hub for knowledge and resource sharing, through networking events and tailored advice. However, to be effective, they would need adequate funding, clear targets, and an efficient human resource policy that encourages network formation and stability.

The Czech government should also consider improving the current network of technology parks and incubators. Czechia has at least 30 science and technology parks (The Science and Technology Parks Association of Czech Republic, 2024[14]) and 30 incubators and accelerators (CzechInvest, 2024[15]). However, the quality of these centres is very heterogenous, as also mentioned in chapter 4. Many of the incubators only offer office space, with limited support in other areas such as test labs, mentorship, and consulting. Encouraging public incubators to provide such services, either in-house or through external experts, will improve the quality of services they provide to SMEs.

Box 5.4. R&D and innovation policies from an EU legislation perspective

Czechia's innovation strategy is broadly in line with European priorities. Both the national and the regional Smart Specialisation Strategies were developed according to the European Commission's Guide to Research and Innovation Strategies for Smart Specialisation (European Commission, 2012[16]). As a result, the domains where Czechia has decided to focus its innovation strategy are also in line with European priorities. Similarly, the innovation domains prioritised in the national Recovery and Resilience Plan (RRP) were established in line with the RIS3 goals and European goals more broadly.

Czechia is also taking part in many European RDI programmes. Czech SMEs can apply to EU-wide proposals organised by the SME Fund, such as the Ideas Powered for business SME Fund. They can apply for Horizon funding, either as part of a consortium or alone, such as in European Innovation Council (EIC) calls. Around 30 projects, either managed or proposed by Czech entities, had received financing from the EIC as of 2024.

Czechia has also tailored some of its innovation funding programmes to match European priorities and requirements. One example is CzechInvest's decision to create sectoral hubs in RIS3 priority areas, aligning its strategy to regional, national and European priorities.

Nevertheless, Czechia could further integrate the European innovation funding system by providing more recognition to certifications such as the European Seal of Excellence. Czechia has used some of the RRP funding to provide financing to EIC Seal of Excellence holders through a programme managed by the Technology Agency of the Czech Republic (TA CR). However, the programme risks losing its funding when the RRP ends in 2027. Ensuring that Seal of Excellence holders have a streamlined procedure for accessing national innovation funds could save administration costs and provide high-quality innovators with the funds needed for development. This recognition could be in the form of a continuation of the existing TA CR programme or a simplification of the requirements for other national programmes. To avoid that this option puts newcomers at a disadvantage, authorities could focus on streamlining the process for winners from past funding rounds. Examples of steps in this direction could include the recognition of past documents, which would avoid duplicating documents for every application, and demanding only minimal documentation relevant for the next step (for instance, showing the future business and innovation plan and how that differs from past performance and funding).

On the other hand, Czechia's SME Support Strategy could be better aligned with the European objectives of RDI investment. In 2021, Czechia's total general expenditure on R&D (GERD) was 2% of GDP, one percentage point below the European Commission's goal of 3% by 2030, and 0.1 percentage point below its own goal of 2.1% by 2021 (Council for Research, Development and Innovation, 2019[17]; European Commission, 2023[18]). Czechia could reach European targets by encouraging both more private and public R&D expenditure.

As seen in this chapter, Czechia could encourage more private RDI expenditure through tax incentives. As of 2024, the SME Strategy only encouraged private R&D activities in general terms, without mentioning the improvement in incentives to invest in such activities (e.g. tax incentives or improvements in the business environment). Czechia could better align with European policies by encouraging the take-up of existing R&D tax incentives by SMEs (see section above) or by developing new ones, heeding the European Commission's encouragement of Member States to provide general tax-based incentives for RDI activities (European Commission, 2023[18]). The establishment of clear targets could further this goal, for instance aiming to double the amount of R&D spending by SMEs by 2030 or increasing SME's use of existing tax incentives and thus reversing the decreasing trend since the mid-2010s.

Czechia could also encourage private innovation more explicitly by providing a framework for regulatory sandboxes. Regulatory sandboxes are regulatory regimes that simplify regulation for new technologies, typically for a limited period, encouraging innovation while ensuring a minimum standard of safety. Examples include the United Kingdom's 2015 regulatory sandbox for FinTech innovation or newer sandboxes that encourage innovation in the area of artificial intelligence (OECD, 2023[19]; Cornelli et al., 2023[20]). The European Commission encourages such sandboxes, as they provide a controlled environment for the development of new technologies (European Commission, 2021[21]; European Commission, 2023[18]).

Conclusions and policy recommendations

Czechia's innovation performance is close to the EU average, but business R&D spending remains relatively low, particularly among SMEs. In 2023, Czechia ranked 14th in the European Commission's Innovation Scoreboard, outperforming other Central and Eastern European countries like Poland, Slovakia and Hungary. However, business R&D spending is below the EU average, with SMEs accounting for only around one-quarter of the total.

Czechia benefits from an integrated innovation strategy thanks to the national Smart Specialisation Strategy, which identifies the main priority technology areas at the national level. Most public institutions involved in innovation policy abide by this prioritisation exercise, which contributes to the overall strategic coherence of government RDI programmes in Czechia.

Public RDI funding has increased in recent years, mostly thanks to external EU sources. External R&D funding rose from 0.44% of GDP in 2017 to 0.61% in 2021, while domestic public funding remained stable at around 0.6% of GDP. However, the proliferation of programmes across multiple funding streams increases complexity and administrative burdens for SMEs. Further streamlining could improve accessibility, although this might require the merger of some of the Czech Operational Programmes, as most public innovation funding comes from EU sources.

Private RDI investment could be further stimulated through more effective tax incentives. The existing R&D tax credit policy does not provide applicants with a strong degree of certainty about the outcome and only benefits profitable firms. Clearer rules and a shift towards a payroll-based R&D tax credit could lower innovation costs, improve liquidity, and strengthen take-up, especially by SMEs. Czechia could also strengthen industry-university linkages by providing more stable funding for technology transfer offices and piloting applied PhD programmes.

Against this backdrop, the following policies could further strengthen the innovation performance of Czech SMEs.

- Streamline existing grant and voucher programmes into fewer larger programmes, including multi-stage funding programmes, to follow innovations and innovators across different technology readiness levels.
- Encourage more private RDI funding, notably by reforming the existing R&D tax credit. Changes would include a more lenient application of the rules defining innovation (and/or a clearer list of eligible costs), a longer carry-forward period (e.g. 5 to 10 years), and changing the tax base of the allowance from corporate income tax to a tax credit on R&D-related labour costs. All these three measures could further favour SMEs through preferential conditions for smaller companies (e.g. longer carry-forward periods).
- Invest more proactively in industry-university knowledge transfer by boosting the funding of technology transfer offices (TTOs) and/or creating a pilot Industrial PhD programme.
- Encourage capacity building for innovation through government-sponsored business consulting services for SMEs and entrepreneurs.
- Continue developing regional innovation centres by ensuring adequate funding and staffing so that these centres can build strong regional innovation systems over time, including by working with universities, technology centres, financiers and other relevant stakeholders.
- Set and monitor clear goals for R&D expenditure by SMEs, consistently with the objectives set in the national innovation strategy.

References

Council for Research, Development and Innovation (2019), *Innovation Strategy of the Czech Republic 2019-2030*, https://www.czechia.eu/wp-content/uploads/2021/11/INNOVATION_STRATEGY_CR_2019-2030_web2.pdf. [17]

Czech Statistical Office (2024), *Tax Support for Research and Development in the Czech Republic 2022.* [9]

Czech Statitistical Office (2022), *Tržby za inovované produkty*, https://csu.gov.cz/docs/107508/49e33d1a-8247-fdfb-7807-2852e5fb373d/21300324a5.pdf?version=1.0. [25]

CzechInvest (2024), *Incubators and Accelerators*, https://www.czechstartups.org/en/startup-ecosystem/incubators-and-accelerators/. [15]

European Commission (2024), *Reciovery and Resilience Scoreboard. Thematic Analysis Research and Innovation*, https://ec.europa.eu/economy_finance/recovery-and-resilience-scoreboard/assets/thematic_analysis/scoreboard_thematic_analysis_research_and_innovation.pdf. [6]

European Commission (2023), *European Innovation Scoreboard 2023*, Publications Office of the European Union, https://data.europa.eu/doi/10.2777/119961. [1]

European Commission (2023), *Long-term competitiveness of the EU: looking beyond 2030*, https://commission.europa.eu/document/af444130-5a3e-44f2-bea6-5b9ddcb46012_en. [18]

European Commission (2021), *Proposal for a Regulation of the European Parliament and of the Council Laying Down Harmonised Rules on Artificial Intelligence (Artificial Intelligence Act) and Amending Certain Union Legislative Acts*, https://eur-lex.europa.eu/legal-content/EN/TXT/?qid=1623335154975&uri=CELEX%3A52021PC0206. [21]

European Commission (2012), *Guide to Research and Innovation Strategies for Smart Specialisation*, https://s3platform.jrc.ec.europa.eu/en/w/guide-on-research-and-innovation-strategies-for-smart-specialisation-ris3-guide-. [16]

Eurydice (2024), *Higher Education Funding in Czechia*, https://eurydice.eacea.ec.europa.eu/national-education-systems/czechia/higher-education-funding. [10]

Grassano, N. et al. (2022), *The 2022 EU Industrial R&D Investment Scoreboard*, https://data.europa.eu/doi/10.2760/08410. [2]

Masaryk University (2024), *Annual Report Masaryk University 2023*, https://www.muni.cz/media/3767418/vyrocni_zprava_o_cinnosti_mu_2023_en.pdf. [24]

Ministry of Industry and Trade (2024), *Final evaluation of the TRIO programme*. [12]

Ministry of Industry and Trade (2024), *National Research and Innovation Strategy. Annex 3 - RIS3 objectives, monitoring indicators and funding*. [7]

OECD (2024), *Strengthening FDI and SME Linkages in Czechia*, OECD Publishing, Paris, https://doi.org/10.1787/4c97d104-en. [4]

OECD (2023), *OECD R&D tax incentives database, 2022 edition*, https://one.oecd.org/document/DSTI/STP/NESTI(2023)2/FINAL/en/pdf. [22]

OECD (2023), *OECD SME and Entrepreneurship Outlook 2023*, OECD Publishing, Paris, https://doi.org/10.1787/342b8564-en. [3]

OECD (2023), “Regulatory sandboxes in artificial intelligence”, *OECD Digital Economy Papers*, No. 356, OECD Publishing, Paris, https://doi.org/10.1787/8f80a0e6-en. [19]

OECD (2021), “Improving knowledge transfer and collaboration between science and business in Spain”, *OECD Science, Technology and Industry Policy Papers*, No. 122, OECD Publishing, Paris, https://doi.org/10.1787/4d787b35-en. [13]

OECD (2015), *Frascati Manual 2015: Guidelines for Collecting and Reporting Data on Research and Experimental Development*, The Measurement of Scientific, Technological and Innovation Activities, OECD Publishing, Paris, https://doi.org/10.1787/9789264239012-en. [5]

Parlour, C. (ed.) (2023), “Regulatory Sandboxes and Fintech Funding: Evidence from the UK”, *Review of Finance*, Vol. 28/1, pp. 203-233, https://doi.org/10.1093/rof/rfad017. [20]

Research, Development and Innovation Council of Czechia (2024), *Evaluation of research organizations and evaluation of programmes of targeted support for research, development and innovation according to the M17+ Methodology*, https://hodnoceni.rvvi.cz/recapitulative-reports/. [11]

Technology Agency of the Czech Republic (2024), *Annual Report 2023*, https://tacr.gov.cz/wp-content/uploads/2024/05/TA-CR_Annual-report-2023_ENG.pdf. [23]

Technology Agency of the Czech Republic (2024), *Programme to Support Applied Research and Innovation SIGMA*, https://tacr.gov.cz/wp-content/uploads/documents/2024/05/07/1715070046_SIGMA%20Programme%20since%207.9.2023.pdf. [8]

The Science and Technology Parks Association of Czech Republic (2024), *Interactive catalog of Science and Technology Parks in Czech Republic*, https://www.svtp.cz/en/. [14]

Notes

[1] The minimum R&D spending required for entering the 2022 EU industrial R&D investment scoreboard was EUR 48.5 million in 2021 (Grassano et al., 2022[2]).

[2] The list of key enabling technologies (KETs) is: (i) photonics and micro/nano electronics, (ii) advanced materials and nanotechnologies, (iii) advanced manufacturing technologies, (iv) life science technologies and biotechnologies, (v) artificial intelligence, and (vi) digital security and connectivity. The list of specialisation domains is (i) advanced materials, technologies, and systems, (ii) digitalisation and automation of manufacturing technologies, (iii) electronics and digital technologies, (iv) environmentally-friendly transport, (v) technologically advanced and safe transport, (vi) advanced medicine and drugs, (vii) cultural and creative industries, (viii) green technologies, bioeconomy and sustainable food sources, (ix) smart cities and municipalities. The full text of Czechia's Smart Specialisation Strategy can be found here: https://www.ris3.cz/sites/default/files/National-RIS3-Strategy_2.pdf.

[3] An example of a call for proposals can be found here: https://www.agentura-api.org/wp-content/uploads/2024/01/inovacni-vouchery-vyzva-i-web-3.pdf.

[4] The implicit tax subsidy rate is defined as 1 minus the B-index. The B-index is the pre-tax income that a representative firm requires to break even of an extra unit of R&D expenditure. A B-index below one suggests that the tax system treats R&D expenditure preferentially, for instance through extra allowances, R&D tax credits or accelerated depreciation. For simplicity, this indicator is usually presented in the form of the implicit subsidy rate, i.e. the difference between a pre-tax income of one euro and the break-even value of the one extra euro of R&D. The higher this value, the higher the subsidy (OECD, 2023[22]).

[5] This is the direction that Czech authorities have chosen. Since 2024, they have broadened the type of evidence that firms can provide to prove that their expenses are meant for R&D.

[6] For instance, in 2023, the Technology Agency had disbursed EUR 237 million in targeted funding for applied research and innovation, with three-quarters (73%) designed to encourage the collaboration between companies and universities and half (54%) aiming to encourage the collaboration between SMEs and universities (Technology Agency of the Czech Republic, 2024[23]). Nevertheless, these funds are relatively small compared to the annual budget of universities. For instance, in 2023, only Masaryk University, Czechia's second largest, had a budget of EUR 400 million, double that of the Technology Agency (Masaryk University, 2024[24]).

[7] The eight performance indicators measure: a) the graduation rate, b) international mobility, c) graduate employment, d) research performance, e) contributions to the arts, f) external revenue, g) studying in a foreign language, and h) the proportion of foreign students.

[8] For more information about Czech firms' innovative activity, see Czech Statitistical Office (2022[25]).

[9] TRLs range from 1 (idea and basic principles) to 9 (full commercial application), with 5 being indicating that a technology has been validated in the relevant environment (e.g., in an industrial environment for KETs). TRLs 4 to 7 are more likely to fall in the "valley of death", as they are too applied for basic research funding and too risky for private financing.

[10] There are already some public procurement for innovation programmes, such as TA CR's BETA programme, but Czechia could consider a more global procurement strategy for encouraging innovation, especially among SMEs.

[11] For more information about the Innovative Solutions Canada, see the programme's Annual Report: https://ised-isde.canada.ca/site/innovative-solutions-canada/en/innovative-solutions-canada-annual-report-2022-23#9

[12] You can find more information on TIPS' website: https://www.jointips.or.kr/about_en.php.

6 SME digitalisation

Czechia has made remarkable progress in improving digital connectivity, although important gaps remain in the diffusion of high-speed broadband. Czech SMEs have also strengthened their digital practices in recent years, although the country's overall performance remains below the EU average. The main national SME digitalisation policy involves the digital innovation hubs, six of which are funded by EU sources. These hubs, both the EU-funded and the others, play a useful role, but they need stabler and longer-term funding for sustained impact. Both the national Recovery and Resilience Plan (RRP) and the Operational Programme "Technology and Applications for Competitiveness" (OP TAC) have SME digitalisation as one of their main objectives, although available budgets are not always up to the challenge. Furthermore, grants and concessional funding could be matched more consistently with soft forms of support, including advisory services and training in digital skills. In this regard, additional actions like awareness-raising campaigns, digitalisation vouchers and online auto-diagnostic tools could further support digital adoption, especially among digital laggards.

Key messages

- While 81% of Czech companies had access to internet speed above 30 Mbit/s in 2023, **the diffusion of high-speed broadband (100 Mbit/s) remains patchy**, especially in rural areas. The country performs well in basic broadband but lags behind in high-speed connections like FTTP & DOCSIS 3.1 standards.
- **Czech SMEs have significantly improved their internet access and digital practices since 2019, although the overall digital performance of the country remains below the EU average**. The EU Digital Economy and Society Index (DESI) ranked Czechia 19th among the 27 EU member states in the business integration of digital technologies in 2022, pointing to slower progress compared to other countries.
- **Czechia has developed a Strategic Plan for Digitalisation which is aligned with current EU goals and focus on the digital transformation of businesses**. Nonetheless, there is scope for a closer alignment between this document and the national SME Support strategy, notably by integrating objectives from the former into the latter.
- **The national Recovery and Resilience Plan (RRP) allocates substantial funding to the digital transition** across different thematic areas such as public administration, cybersecurity, and education. Business-related funding amounts to EUR 662 million, which may fall short of addressing key barriers such as high technology costs and existing skills gaps in SMEs.
- **Czechia has six European Digital Innovation Hubs (EDIHs)** which are co-funded by EU sources and offer services in digital skills, innovation, and access to funding opportunities. **These hubs face funding challenges**, as current arrangements cover only up to 2026, **and would require stable, long-term funding for sustained impact**. The government could also consider backing additional hubs across the country, possibly through a mixed-funding approach combining public and private resources.
- **Three main grant schemes under the Operational Programme "Technology and Applications for Competitiveness" (OP TAC) support SME digitalisation**: a) Digital Enterprise; b) Virtual Enterprise, and c) Technology 4.0. These schemes are well-received but need broader outreach and complementary business development services to address the delay in SME digital adoption. In this regard, additional actions like awareness-raising campaigns, coaching, training, digitalisation vouchers and online auto-diagnostic tools could further support adoption, especially by digital laggards.
- **Finally, Czechia has made important strides in the digitalisation of its public administration.** Digital interactions between the government and the private sector can be used as a leverage to support business digitalisation efforts.

SME digitalisation conditions

There have been improvements in the digital infrastructure, but the diffusion of high-speed broadband is still patchy

Digitalisation is a key enabler of business success, for example by enabling better access to markets or by supporting the green transition. However, business digitalisation also depends, to some degree, on the quality of the national digital infrastructure.

Czechia's digital infrastructure has improved over the last years. In 2023, 81% of Czech companies had a fixed internet connection speed of more than 30 Mbit/s, a proportion that has steadily increased in recent years. However, coverage at 100 Mbit/sec shows many gaps, especially in rural areas. Only about half of Czech businesses (45% in 2023) are connected to the Internet at a speed higher than 100 Mbit/s, which is up from 34.5% in 2020, but still lower than many other European countries (Figure 6.1, Panel A).[1]

FTTP & DOCSIS 3.1 are 1Gbps-capable networks and broadly correspond to high-speed broadband access or "superfast internet". While Czechia scores better than most of the other EU27 countries in the coverage of fixed and NGA broadband, which can be considered as "low-speed" Internet, the overall FTTP & DOCSIS 3.1 coverage in rural areas is far below the average (Figure 6.1, Panel B).

Figure 6.1. Internet coverage in Czechia, 2022

Panel A: The map of Czechia with internet coverage at 100 Mbit/sec, 2022	Panel B: Coverage by technology combination in Czechia and the EU27 average, Percentage values, 2022

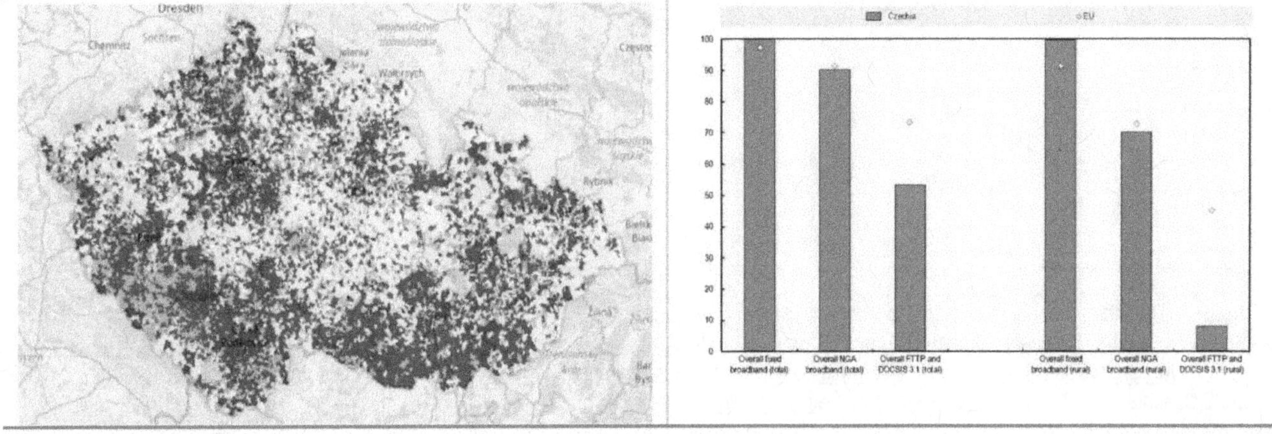

Source: https://apps.bconetwork.cz/MAPA/mapa_GSD2022.html and https://digital-strategy.ec.europa.eu/en/library/broadband-coverage-europe-2022

The digital skills of the adult population have also improved

Digital skills are also instrumental to a successful digital transition of the business sector. In Czechia, 70% of the population aged 16- 74 had at least basic digital skills in 2023, which is significantly higher than the EU average (56%). In 2021, the figures for Czechia and the EU-27 were respectively 60% and 54%, making Czechia one of the EU countries with fastest progress in this area.[2]

SME digitalisation is gaining steam

Czech enterprises have experienced increasingly better access to the Internet, although the share of companies with fast connection is still low, which reflects the abovementioned delays in digital infrastructure development. Similarly, the adoption of digital practices, such as the purchase of cloud computing services or the use of social media for business purposes, has also increased over time (see Figure 6.2, Panel A).

Nonetheless, Czechia still ranked 19th out of the 27 EU member states in the integration of digital technologies by businesses. Information from the EU Digital Economy and Society Index (DESI) also shows that Czech enterprises do better than the EU average in areas like the use of cloud computing services and e-commerce, while they lag behind in the use of ICT for environmental sustainability purposes and electronic invoices (Figure 6.2, Panel B).

Figure 6.2. The digitalisation of Czech enterprises

Percentage values

Panel A: Access to the Internet and digital practices, 2016-2023

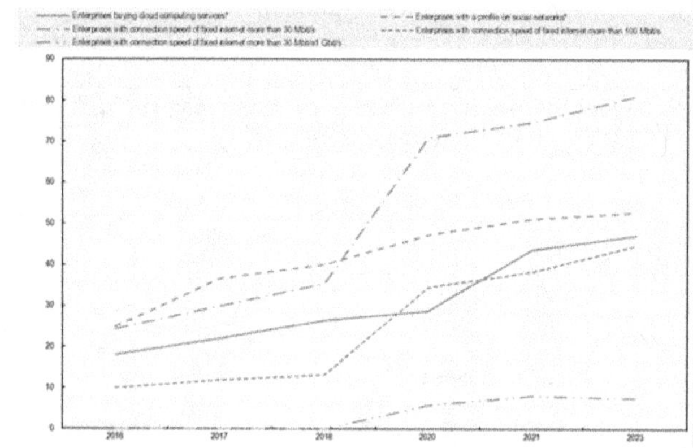

Panel B: Integration of digital technologies by firms, 2022

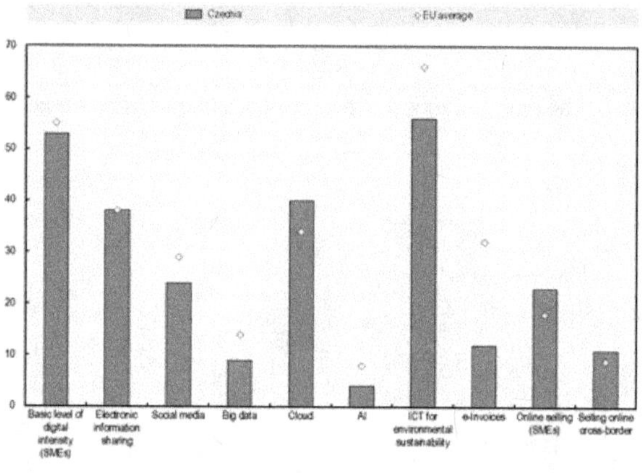

Note: (*) The indicator only covers enterprises with at least 10 employees
Source: Czech Statistical Office, ICT in enterprises, https://csu.gov.cz/ict-in-enterprises?pocet=10&start=0&podskupiny=403&razeni=-datumVydani#data-and-time-series__enterprises-using-selected-digital-technology & Digital Economy and Society Index (DESI) 2022,Czechia, https://digital-strategy.ec.europa.eu/en/policies/desi-czech-republic

Similar results are shown by the European Investment Bank (EIB), which finds that a slightly higher percentage of Czech firms use advanced digital technologies compared to the EU average. The EIB study also points out that the likelihood of using digital technologies increases with firm size and that the main digitalisation barriers experienced by Czech SMEs include gaps in the digital infrastructure, in line with the previous section, and a shortage of digital skills, which seems to be in conflict with the abovementioned improvements in the digital skills of the population (European Investment Bank, 2020[1]).

According to Eurostat, 20.5% of all Czech companies with at least ten employees showed either high or very high digital intensity in 2021[3]. In 2023, the proportion rose slightly to 21.0%. For the EU 27 average, the numbers were 22.1% and 25.2% respectively, indicating slowee progress in Czechia than in the rest of the EU. Finally, still at the EU level, the 2024 Digital Decade Country Report for Czechia, which is part of the EU 2030 Digital Decade framework, highlights gaps in SME digitalisation, particularly in the adoption of AI, cloud services, data analytics, and digital skills. The report recommends increased skills training and SME support to overcome these obstacles (European Commission, 2024[2]).

Overall, these figures offer a picture of a country where there has been progress in digitalisation over the last years, but where more can be done to strengthen the digital infrastructure and to foster the use of digital technologies and practices by SMEs.

The OP EIC, forerunner of the current OP TAC, provides some lessons for current SME digitalisation policies

The Operational Programme "Enterprise and Innovation for Competitiveness" (OP EIC), which is the precursor of the current OP TAC (Operational Programme Technologies and Application for Competitiveness), has been instrumental in promoting SME digitalisation in Czechia and offers some lessons for current SME digitalisation programmes. Through targeted funding programmes, the OP EIC aimed to enhance SMEs' digital infrastructure, IT capabilities, and overall competitiveness. Key initiatives included the "ICT and Shared Services" Programme and the "Enterprise Digitalisation" Call, which provided SMEs with financial support to modernise operations and adopt new digital solutions.

The ICT and Shared Services Programme stood out as the primary digitalisation support within OP EIC, targeting the development of new ICT products, data centre construction, and shared service facilities. The programme had approved a substantial number of projects by 2022, about 600, of which 352 projects focused on creating ICT solutions. This programme effectively boosted SMEs' access to advanced digital tools and services but also faced some challenges. Many SMEs found the application processes complex which, combined with limited administrative capacity, affected the completion rate of projects.

The Enterprise Digitalisation Call, on the other hand, focused explicitly on accelerating digitalisation in SME operations through supporting automation, cloud adoption, and data management. This call attracted 153 projects, although only a small fraction had been fully implemented by 2022, which suggests the need of streamlining project-related procedures and providing additional support to businesses to ensure the timely execution of projects.

The Recovery and Resilience Plan has a strong focus on digitalisation, including business digitalisation

Czechia's Recovery and Resilience Plan (RRP) was approved in July 2021 with a total budget of EUR 9.2 billion (with EUR 8.4 billion in grants and the remaining EUR 818 in loans). It includes significant measures to foster the digital transition, with 23% of the budget allocated to this endeavour. A modified plan was accepted in October 2023 and shifted even more resources into the digital transition (from 21% to 23% of the total). All measures must be implemented with a tight timeline, as the regulation establishing the RRP requires all milestones and targets to be achieved by August 2026. The actions of the RRP in the realm of digitalisation can be broken down into five different areas, namely:

- Investments and reforms in digital skills, e-government, digital connectivity, and business digital transformation.
- Investments in digital equipment for schools, training for teachers, new university programmes in fast-growing digital fields, and upskilling and reskilling for citizens (EUR 585 million)
- Construction of university infrastructure (EUR 368 million).
- Investments in cyber-security and the digital transformation of public administration, the justice system and health care (EUR 790 million).
- The digital transformation of businesses, digital innovation hubs and very high-capacity networks and 5G networks (EUR 662 million).[4]

The RRP has, therefore, a broad digitalisation agenda, whereas this chapter only covers the digital transformation of businesses. In this subfield, the main objective of the RRP has been to support the improvement of the digital level of SMEs operating in domestic and foreign markets, which is achieved by supporting the adoption of advanced non-production technologies such as automation, AI, and big data.

Both the RRP and the National RIS3 Strategy (smart specialisation strategy) share this focus. In particular, RRP projects must align with the Specific Objective D0.1 of the National RIS3 Strategy, which promotes the digitalisation and use of new technologies in businesses, ensuring that initiatives funded through the RRP also contribute to longer-term national innovation goals.

While Czechia's RRP reflects a strong commitment to the digital transformation, some challenges raised in recent evaluations need consideration. In particular, although the budget of EUR 662 million dedicated to business digitalisation is significant, these resources may fall short of overcoming key barriers such as high technology costs and existing digital skills gaps. Furthermore, there also seems to be a lack of attention in the RRP to the development of soft skills like change management, which are crucial for the adoption of new technologies.

The European Digital Innovation Hubs are the main national SME digitalisation policy

Czechia's main SME digitalisation initiative is the European Digital Innovation Hubs (EDIH), with six of them that are spread across the country. These are one-stop shops assisting the business sector and the public administration in addressing digital challenges and are co-financed by the European Commission and the national government. All of them have received support from the Digital Europe Programme and the National Recovery Plan (each at a rate of 50%), with a total amount of CZK 428 million (around EUR 17 million).

Half of these hubs provide expertise on specific digital technologies to companies across the country, such as Artificial Intelligence (AI) or cybersecurity, while the remaining half cater to the needs of companies within specific regions. All of them provide services in a standard four-pillar structure:

- Test-before-invest: The hubs own physical and technological infrastructure where clients can test digital technologies before investing in the acquisition. As one example, the EDIH Ostrava (located in the capital city of the Moravian-Silesian Region) offers a core facility of High-Performance Computing (HPC), complemented by an experimental industrial testbed[5];
- Access to investment and funding: The hubs facilitate access to finance for SMEs by providing information, advisory services, and networking opportunities. They organise workshops, seminars, and matchmaking events to educate and connect SMEs with potential investors. EDIHs also assist with financial planning, strategy development, and preparation of funding proposals. They help SMEs navigate European funding opportunities and enter into collaborative projects.
- Education and digital skills: In this case, an example is given by DIH "Brain 4 Industry" (B4I), which has set up an academy offering 13 courses, ranging from basic introductions to advanced and expert courses.[6]
- Innovation ecosystems and networking: EDIHs connect their clients to research institutions, specialised business clusters, professional organisations, and public administrations on a need basis.

Interviews from the project's fact-finding mission indicate that Czechia's EDIHs are a novel feature of the policy support landscape and are currently in full expansion. The services offered to the clients are (typically) free of charge, and a large majority of clients are SMEs, alongside various public authorities. All five EDIHs that have been subject to a formal evaluation have received a positive assessment by the European Commission (European Commission - Joint Research Centre, 2024[3]). They are also part of the Network of European Digital Innovation Hubs, a platform enabling the sharing of good practices among all 228 EDIHs at the EU level[7].

In addition to the six officially recognised European Digital Innovation Hubs, there are seven other similar structures operating in Czechia. These hubs do not receive direct funding from the Digital Europe Programme and are not part of the EU-backed network, but they still play a crucial role in supporting SMEs and public organisations in digitalisation nationwide. These non-EU funded hubs often rely on a combination of national, regional, and private funding and provide services according to regional needs. For instance, some hubs initially started operations under EU funding programmes like Horizon 2020 and have continued to operate with a thematic focus, whether it be sector- or technology-based.[8]

The Digital Innovation Hubs will need stable funding

Czechia's EDIHs appear to be working well and are well aligned with the strategy developed by the European Commission to support SME digitalisation, in which EDIHs are one of the pillars. Although no formal statistics about SME uptake are yet available, it appears that the target of reaching 200 SMEs through these hubs will easily be achieved.

Nonetheless, funding arrangements have been made only up to 2026, and the funding is very reliant on EU sources. It would be important that these structures remain in place afterwards, especially because it takes years for such organisations to be fully operational at scale. Stable funding allows for long-term planning, which is key to achieving significant sustained impacts. The government should therefore find long-term funding solutions for these centres, possibly through multi-annual budgets and additional financing mechanisms, such as funding from regional governments, private sector contributions (for instance by charging the beneficiaries for some of the services provided) and participation in EU projects. Across EU countries, mixed funding models, in which EU financing is complemented with regional and national sources, are common and, in fact, are becoming increasingly prevalent (European Investment Bank, 2020[1]).

The reported budget per EDIH per year also appears to be relatively small and could be increased to make even further the digital innovation hubs the main linchpin of national SME digitalisation policies. While the budget of EDIHs varies significantly and depends on many variables, such as the nature of technology infrastructures and testing facilities, the average budget appears to be between EUR 2-3 million. Moreover, the demand for their services outstrips the supply, which is an indication that the programmes and services delivered are of good quality and could be scaled up.

The number of Digital Innovation Hubs could be increased to reach more SMEs

In addition to the six digital innovation hubs that receive funding from the EU level, there are seven other similar centres active in the country, which do not have stable revenues other than the income from the offer of their services at commercial rates[9]. These hubs would also merit stable and predictable income sources, ideally combining public funding with private streams of income.

This is all the more desirable because other EU countries with a roughly comparable population have a larger number of digital innovation hubs to drive SME digitalisation efforts (see Table 6.1). Czech EDIHs primarily focus on the digitisation of production processes, engineering, and cybersecurity, while they have less emphasis on digitising sectors like transport, energy, and healthcare. Other potentially important areas for SMEs such as personal services, consumer products, and construction are also neglected or receive small attention, despite these areas being targeted by digital innovation hubs in other EU member states. This gap presents significant opportunities for establishing and promoting additional hubs in Czechia to address overlooked sectors and technologies, keeping in mind that EU member states can, and often do, complement EU-level funding with national funding to establish and operate additional digital hubs.

Table 6.1. Digital innovation hubs in Czechia and selected EU countries, 2022

Country	Population (million)	Digital Innovation Hubs
Czechia	10.2	13
Belgium	11.6	29
Hungary	9.7	10
Portugal	10.3	8
Austria	8.9	15
Greece	10.7	16
Sweden	10.4	17

Source: Samek (2022), Methodology for the Development of Innovation Infrastructures in the Czech Republic: System support for the implementation and management of the National RIS3, https://www.mpo.gov.cz/assets/cz/podnikani/ris3-strategie/projekty-na-podporu-ris3/operacni-program-vyzkum-vyvoj-a-vzdelavani/2023/2/Metodika-rozvoje-inovacnich-infrastruktur-v-CR.pdf.

The government could give more attention to "soft" forms of support, such as online diagnostic tools

Three calls part of the Operational Programme "Technologies and Application for Competitiveness" (OP TAC) have been developed to support SME digitalisation, namely[10]:

- Digital Enterprise: This is a grant scheme supporting the purchase and introduction of advanced non-production digital technologies.[11] The subsidy amounts to CZK 1.5-15 million with 30 to 60% covered by the scheme (dependent on both the size and location of the beneficiary). The project must result in a shift in digitalisation: the applicant must meet at least 7 of the 12 DESI digital technology objectives by the end of the project.
- Virtual Enterprise is a similar scheme whereby the investment must be linked to a significant shift toward digitalisation. It provides a subsidy of CZK 0.5-5 million, with 30-60% covered by the scheme (dependent on both the size and location of the beneficiary).[12]
- Technology 4.0: It supports SME transformation of business models through digital technologies. The subsidy amounts to CZK 5-50 million with 30 to 60% covered by the scheme (dependent on both the size and location of the beneficiary).[13]

During the fact-finding mission of the project, it was reported that these instruments have approximately an uptake of 600 each and work well, covering a broad spectrum of Czech SMEs in need of financial support to invest in digital technologies. While it is too early to formally assess the impact of these schemes, it seems likely that they will contribute to the specific objectives of the National SME Support Strategy to "increase the use of digital tools and new technologies in SMEs". Nonetheless, the uptake of some of these programmes, notably Virtual Enterprise, is relatively modest given the large number of SMEs that are currently not employing digital tools and technologies and the digitalisation targets set by the Czech Government.

Furthermore, the use of subsidies could be complemented by "softer approaches" that focus more on how to use digital technologies in addition to covering part of the costs. The evaluation exercise of the previous OP EIC programmes, for example, referred to the benefit of complementing financial aid with softer forms of support, possibly through dedicated competence centres (European Commission, 2024[4]). While the EDIHs provide these services as part of their portfolio, their outreach has been limited. Similarly, regional innovation centres sometimes offer such programmes (see Box 6.1), but these centres only exist in seven of the fourteen Czech regions, and their scope and range of services is very different depending on the location.

Box 6.1. Business development services for SME digitalisation in the Olomouc region

ICOK DIGI is a programme from the Olomouc Region that aims to increase the level of digital transformation of local companies. The programme includes the elaboration of an initial process analysis, including a proposal for a solution, a series of consultations with an independent expert, and participation in workshops aimed at sharing good-practice examples. The interventions are tailored to the specific needs of the company and are based on its level of digital maturity. The project also seeks to set up a long-term strategy for the entire digitisation process of the company and related key activities.

In parallel with tailored consultations, workshops are organised to help attract attention, drawing companies into the issue of digitalisation. Business representatives can also test whether specific technologies or processes are relevant to their business before they decide to eventually invest in the acquisition of specific technologies.

Source: https://www.inovaceok.cz/sluzba/digi

Therefore, there may be scope for additional actions to effectively digitalise small companies in Czechia, especially digital laggards. Some OECD countries have developed comprehensive approaches that, besides grant support and digital hubs or similar structures, include:[14]

- Awareness-raising campaigns: Czechia could do more in this area besides the annual Industry Cluster 4.0 conference, which takes place in February every year.
- Digital skills and "soft skills" training programmes for SME owners and managers: These could include online courses, workshops, and in-house training sessions and would require close collaboration with educational institutions, universities and technical schools offering practical training and certification programmes tailored to SME needs. Survey data from the Association of Small and Medium-Sized Enterprises and Crafts (AMSP ČR) (Box 6.3) indicate, for example, that the lack of internal expertise or knowledge is the main single barrier facing Czech firms that want to digitalise.
- Digitalisation vouchers: These are well suited to the needs of SMEs at the beginning of their digital journey and could serve various objectives besides digitalisation, including the improvement of management skills. An example is Spain's Digital Kit Voucher Scheme.
- Online diagnostic tools: Online diagnostic tools offer a cost-effective and accessible way for policymakers to engage with businesses that are otherwise difficult to reach. These tools generally allow firms to benchmark their performance across various metrics, helping them identify potential areas for improvement. Typically, they also provide guidance on how to address identified weaknesses and direct businesses to relevant support initiatives.

Figure 6.3. Challenges faced by Czech companies during the digitalisation process, 2023

Percentage values

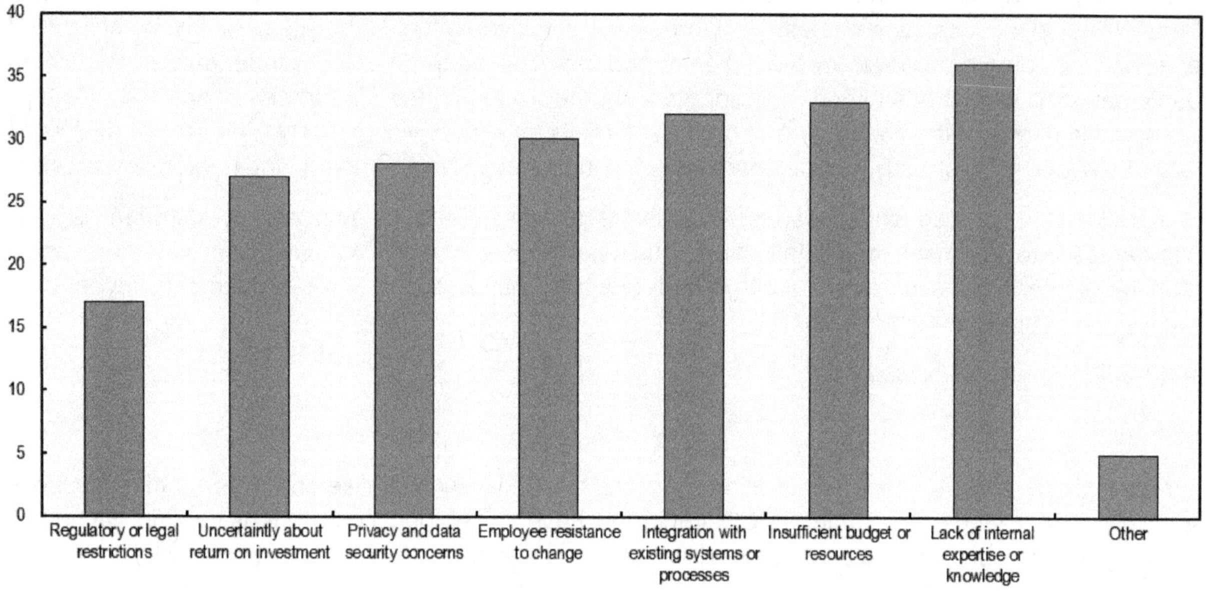

Note: Based on responses by 202 Czech companies with between 5 and 249 employees to an online survey by the Association of Small and Medium-sized Enterprises and Tradesmen of the Czech Republic, submitted in May 2023.
Source: https://amsp.cz/wp-content/uploads/2023/09/DIGI-a-KYBER-FINAL-pruzkum.pdf

Auto-diagnostic tools, in particular, can target different aspects that are crucial for SME performance, such as productivity and innovation. For instance, the "Canada Business Productivity" tool by the Business Development Bank of Canada focuses on productivity, while "COTEC Portugal" emphasises innovation. Firms can benchmark and compare their performance with peers, which helps them identify areas that need improvement. These tools also provide actionable insights and link businesses to relevant support programmes. Czech authorities could consider the development of a similar auto-diagnostic tool. This tool could either be part of a broader toolkit addressing various SME performance aspects or exclusively focus on SME digitalisation. Bpifrance's *Digitalomètre*, a toolkit developed by France's public development bank, offers an example (Box 6.2) (OECD, 2021[5])[15].

Box 6.2. The Digital meter (*Digitalomètre*) of Bpifrance

Bpifrance, France's public investment bank, has developed *Digitalomètre*, an innovative online self-diagnostic tool supporting SME digitalisation. *Digitalomètre* is a free online questionnaire designed to be easily accessible to all SMEs. The user-friendly interface ensures that even businesses with limited digital experience can navigate and complete the assessment. The questionnaire takes approximately 15 minutes to complete, making it a quick and efficient way for businesses to assess their digital maturity without significant time investment.

The tool evaluates various aspects of digital maturity, including digital skills, technology use, online presence, and cybersecurity practices. This comprehensive approach helps businesses gain a holistic understanding of their digital capabilities. Upon completion, businesses receive a detailed report highlighting their digital strengths and weaknesses. The tool provides tailored recommendations for improvement, guiding SMEs in their digital transformation journey.

Digitalomètre allows businesses to benchmark their digital maturity against industry standards and peers. This comparative analysis helps SMEs understand where they stand in the digital landscape and identify areas for competitive improvement. The tool links businesses to relevant support programmes and initiatives, which can be offered by Bpifrance as well as other partners. This integration ensures that SMEs not only identify their digital needs but also have access to the resources required to address such needs.

Source: (OECD, 2021[5]) & « *Evaluez votre maturité digitale avec le Digitalomètre* », https://www.bpifrance.fr/nos-actualites/evaluez-votre-maturite-digitale-avec-le-digitalometre

Initiatives to digitalise the interactions between the public administration and SMEs can also support business digitalisation

The Strategic Plan for the Digitalisation of Czechia outlines various measures that can contribute to the digital transformation of businesses. One key initiative is the Digital and Information Agency (DIA), whose main role consists in expanding eGovernment services and ensuring inter-operability between state administration and private-sector digital tools. For example, the expansion of data mailboxes (*Datové schránky*), now mandatory for legal entities, facilitates faster, fully digital communication between businesses and government institutions, reducing paperwork and administrative costs. Similarly, the *Moje Daně* (My Taxes) Portal has modernised tax filing, making compliance easier for SMEs by integrating online tax reporting and digital payments. While these initiatives go in the right direction, further actions to strengthen the connection between the digitalisation of the public sector and SME digitalisation could include pairing every new government mandatory digital service with simple onboarding materials and the government partnering with technology providers to offer affordable tools to SMEs.

Box 6.3. SME digitalisation policies from an EU legislation perspective

The European Commission (EC) has established several key documents and strategies to support SME digitalisation. The "2030 Digital Compass: the European way for the Digital Decade" is of the most prominent (European Commission, 2021[6]). The resulting Digital Decade Policy Programme (DDPP) aims to operationalise the ambitions of the Compass and has a focus on skills, infrastructure, government and, most relevant for this evaluation report, businesses, with three targets set for 2030:

- Tech up-take: 75% of EU companies using Cloud, AI, or Big Data.
- Innovators: Doubling the number of EU Unicorns, including through enhanced offer of scale-up finance.
- Late adopters: more than 90% of SMEs reaching at least a basic level of digital intensity.

So far, two reports have been released to assess progress towards the objectives of the Digital Decade Roadmap (European Commission, 2024[7]). The main message is that, at the EU level, greater efforts are needed to reach the EU ambitions on all four dimensions of the Compass: skills, infrastructure, government, and businesses. The update of the Czech roadmap was also approved in January 2025.

The Czech Government has aligned its policies with the main EU digitalisation strategies, including through the national RRP, the OP TAC programmes, and the digital innovation hubs, which have all been discussed earlier.

However, the digitalisation goals of the National Digital Decade Strategic Roadmap and the national SME Support Strategy, appear to be disconnected. In particular, the former sets specific, measurable targets like increasing cloud usage and AI adoption among businesses, which are not reflected in the SME Support Strategy. The two national strategic documents could therefore be better aligned, for example by replicating the objectives of the National Roadmap into the SME Support Strategy, especially the following ones:

- Raise the proportion of businesses that use cloud services from 40% in 2021 to 60% by 2030.
- Raise the proportion of businesses that perform big data analysis from 9.12% in 2020 to 35% by 2030.
- Raise the proportion of businesses that use one or more artificial intelligence technologies from 5% in 2021 to 21% by 2030.
- Raise the proportion of businesses with a least a basic level of digital intensity from 68% in 2022 to 80% by 2030.
- Raise the number of unicorns active in Czechia from 4 in 2022 to 6 by 2030.

Conclusions and policy recommendations

Czechia has made notable progress in expanding digital infrastructure and supporting SME digitalisation, but important gaps still remain. While most firms now benefit from basic broadband access, high-speed connections, which are crucial for advanced digital applications, are still unevenly deployed, particularly in rural areas. SMEs have improved their digital practices in recent years, but the country's slower progress in adopting advanced technologies is reflected in its middling EU ranking in digital adoption indicators. Existing support programmes, such as the European Digital Innovation Hubs and OP TAC grant schemes, offer valuable services but require broader outreach, long-term funding stability, and complementary initiatives – e.g., awareness campaigns, coaching, and diagnostic tools – to maximise their impact, especially among lagging SMEs. Continued improvements in digital public administration also present an opportunity to reinforce business digitalisation efforts, helping Czech companies fully harness the benefits of the digital transition.

Against this backdrop, the main policy recommendations to enhance SME digitalisation in Czechia include:

- Aligning the digitalisation objectives of the SME Strategy with the business digitalisation objectives of the Strategic Plan for the Digitalisation of Czechia.
- Moving ahead with plans to address gaps in the national coverage of high-speed broadband, especially in rural and peripheral areas of the country.
- Increasing outreach and awareness efforts, especially towards digital laggards, many of which are smaller SMEs, in collaboration with local business associations.
- Complementing grant support with business development services, such as skills training and workshops, consultancy services and mentorship programmes.
- Establishing a diversified and stable source of income for the digital innovation hubs, both those funded by the Digital Europe Programme and those that are not. In this respect, it is also important to ensure that digital innovation hubs operate at sufficient scale and cover most relevant thematic areas and regions of Czechia.
- Developing an auto-diagnostic tool that allows Czech firms to assess their "digital readiness" in an accessible and standardised manner.
- Piloting a digital voucher scheme, whereby selected SMEs can receive small funding for simple digitalisation services and technologies, assessing its impact after 3-5 years, and adjusting the scheme accordingly.

- Leveraging the digitalisation of the public administration to encourage more SMEs to take up digital technologies.

References

Czech Republic – Ministry of Industry and Trade (2014), *Ex-ante Evaluation of the Operational Programme Enterprise and Innovation for Competitiveness 2014 – 2020*, Ministry of Industry and Trade, Prague. [9]

European Commission (2024), *2030 Digital Decade: Report on the state of the digital decade 2024*, European Commission, Brussels. [7]

European Commission (2024), *Czechia 2024 Digital Decade Country Report*. [2]

European Commission (2024), *Study supporting the ex post evaluation of the Entrepreneurship and Innovation Programme (EIP) 2007-2013*, European Commission, Brussels. [4]

European Commission (2021), *2030 Digital Compass: the European way for the Digital Decade*. [6]

European Commission - Joint Research Centre (2024), *European Digital Innovation Hubs Network's activities and customers*, EC - JRC. [3]

European Investment Bank (2020), *Financing the digitalisation of small and medium-sized enterprises: The enabling role of digital innovation hubs*, European Investment Bank, Luxembourg. [1]

OECD (2021), *SME and Entrepreneurship Policy in the Slovak Republic*, OECD Studies on SMEs and Entrepreneurship, OECD Publishing, Paris, https://doi.org/10.1787/9097a251-en. [5]

Samek (2022), *Methodology for the Development of Innovation Infrastructures in the Czech Republic: System support for the implementation and management of the National RIS*, Czech Ministry of Industry and Trade. [8]

Notes

[1] See: https://csu.gov.cz/ict-in-enterprises?pocet=10&start=0&podskupiny=403&razeni=-datumVydani

[2] See: Eurostat, "How many citizens had basic digital skills in 2021?", 30 March 2022, https://ec.europa.eu/eurostat/web/products-eurostat-news/-/ddn-20220330-1.

[3] Business digital intensity is defined by the degree by which businesses use digital technologies and services in their operations.

[4] See website of the Czech Recovery and Resilience Plan: https://commission.europa.eu/business-economy-euro/economic-recovery/recovery-and-resilience-facility/country-pages/czechias-recovery-and-resilience-plan_en

[5] For further information, see: https://european-digital-innovation-hubs.ec.europa.eu/edih-catalogue/edih-ova.

[6] See: https://academy.brain4industry.cz/kurzy/

[7] For further information, see: https://european-digital-innovation-hubs.ec.europa.eu/home.

[8] An overview of existing digital innovation hubs in Czechia is available at the following page: "Czech Digital Innovation Hubs: who are they and how can they help?", https://robohub.org/czech-digital-innovation-hubs-who-are-they-and-how-can-they-help/.

[9] See: Samek (2022), Methodology for the Development of Innovation Infrastructures in the Czech Republic: System support for the implementation and management of the National RIS3, https://www.mpo.gov.cz/assets/cz/podnikani/ris3-strategie/projekty-na-podporu-ris3/operacni-program-vyzkum-vyvoj-a-vzdelavani/2023/2/Metodika-rozvoje-inovacnich-infrastruktur-v-CR.pdf

[10] OP TAC, which is funded by the ERDF, does not support companies based in the Prague.

[11] "Non-production" relates to business functions outside the direct manufacturing or production processes. These include technologies that enhance business operations, management, and digital infrastructure rather than physical production such as Enterprise Resource Planning (ERP) systems or Customer Relationship Management (CRM) tools.

[12] Further information at: https://www.agentura-api.org/wp-content/uploads/2023/06/digitalni-podnik-vyzva-i-cs-en-gb-c.pdf

[13] Further information at: https://www.agentura-api.org/wp-content/uploads/2023/11/digitalni-podnik-technologie-4.0-vyzva-i-1.pdf.

[14] Examples include Spain (Go Digital Programme), Germany (Mittelstand-Digital Programme) and the United Kingdom (Digital Boost Initiative). While these initiatives differ one from the other, they share a strong focus on raising awareness among SMEs (including those that are not at the digital forefront) and providing soft support measures on how to digitalise.

[15] See: https://www.bpifrance.fr/nos-actualites/evaluez-votre-maturite-digitale-avec-le-digitalometre. Other examples with an online auto-diagnostic toolkit specific for SME digitalisation include Spain (https://www.acelerapyme.es/quieres-conocer-el-grado-de-digitalizacion-de-tu-pyme), Belgium's Wallonia (https://www.1890.be/solution/les-outils-gratuits-de-digital-wallonia-pour-mesure-votre-maturite-numerique/), and Canada (https://www.bdc.ca/en/articles-tools/entrepreneur-toolkit/business-assessments/digital-maturity)..

7 The green transition of SMEs

Czechia has made meaningful progress in decarbonising its economy, notably by lowering energy intensity and expanding renewable energy sources. Nonetheless, it remains one of the most energy-intensive EU countries due to its large manufacturing base and continued reliance on coal in electricity generation. SMEs account for an estimated 41–48% of business-sector GHG emissions, yet only a small share have adopted climate strategies. Those that do, however, also introduce specific climate actions, such as developing or acquiring new environmental technologies.

Government support for improved energy efficiency in SMEs is substantial through the offer of both financing and advisory services. However, the national energy audit system needs to be strengthened, and there is scope for streamlining the existing fragmented offer of energy advisory services into one single flagship initiative with a larger budget and stronger visibility to the SME targeted audience. Smaller government schemes have also encouraged the uptake of renewable energy sources and the adoption of circular-economy practices in SMEs. However, given the high material intensity of the Czech economy, financial support for the SME adoption of circularity could be scaled up. Finally, the Czech government could devote more attention to green skills development, especially in its three coal mining regions, and to supporting SME compliance with sustainability reporting requirements.

Key messages

- **Czechia has made progress in decarbonising its national economy by reducing energy intensity and by increasing the share of renewables in the national energy mix. However, it is still one of the most energy-intensive countries in the EU**, which is a consequence of the comparatively larger weight of manufacturing in the economy and the relatively wide use of coal in electricity generation. Furthermore, despite a 42% drop in material intensity since 2000, Czechia still lags behind the EU average across the main resource-efficiency indicators.
- **Czech SMEs account for between 41-48% of business-sector greenhouse (GHG) emissions, in line with the EU average. Survey evidence also shows that only 14% of SMEs had a climate strategy in place, compared with 21% at the EU level**. Nevertheless, those Czech SMEs that have a climate strategy in place are more green-active than European peers, with 58% of them developing and 66% of them purchasing new green technologies. Among the main barriers to undertaking resource-efficiency actions, Czech SMEs were more likely to report the complexity of administrative and legal procedures (49%), complex environmental reporting requirements (34%), and the costs associated with environmental actions (26%).
- **The Czech government has actively supported energy efficiency in the business sector through a suite of programmes** (e.g., Energy Savings, ENERG-ETS, and the Transformation Loans). **However, the national energy audit system would benefit from reforms**, notably by ensuring that energy audits are effectively followed by concrete energy-saving actions.
- **National energy consulting services (e.g., EKIS and EnKoMas) offer valuable free advice to help SMEs improve their energy performance.** However, the current offer looks fragmented and could be streamlined into one single flagship programme with a larger budget and better visibility to the SME targeted audience.
- **Czechia has encouraged the uptake of renewable energy sources (RES) by SMEs**, including through a project call of the Ministry of Industry and Trade (MIT) supporting the installation of solar panels and the purchase of batteries by SMEs which has led to a 14% progress towards the 2030 objective of installed photovoltaic capacity by SMEs. Furthermore, legislative changes have enabled smaller energy producers (from 10 kWh to 50 kWh) to operate without a license, thus further facilitating RES development, in particular solar power.
- Czechia lags behind the EU average in the registration of new electric vehicles (EV). In this area, **the Electromobility Guarantee Programme has encouraged the acquisition of EVs by SMEs through a financial contribution and a loan guarantee.** While the programme has been well-received, supporting the acquisition of over 5 300 EVs and 2 200 charging stations within the first six months, its benefits are possibly too generous. The Czech government could, therefore, consider a revised version of the programme that reaches more companies through a smaller subsidy rate.
- **Recent calls under OP TAC have also encouraged SMEs to improve the circularity of their business operations**, notably through better recycling, re-use of material and product eco-design. **Going forward, given the high material intensity of the Czech economy, financial support could be scaled up.** Furthermore, advisory services, adequate legislation and better recycling infrastructure are also important to ensure that businesses can effectively adopt circular-economy practices.
- **The Czech government could develop a more systemic approach to green skills development,** covering education and training programmes for high, mid- and low-skilled workers, as well as the monitoring of green skills demand to ensure that the current training offer is in step with labour market trends.

- **Finally, the Czech government could support SMEs in their compliance efforts with sustainability reporting requirements.** While the European Sustainability Reporting Standards (ESRS) introduced by the Corporate Sustainability Reporting Directive (CSRD) do not directly affect SMEs, there are concerns that SMEs will be impacted indirectly through their relationships with financial institutions and large companies, which are subject to the obligations of the CSRD. The government could offer help through advisory services – for example, on the voluntary SME reporting standards currently being prepared at the EU level – and through the development of automated reporting mechanisms allowing the sharing of emissions-related company information between authorised public and private entities.

SME greening conditions

Czechia is one of the most carbon-intensive economies in the EU, partly due to the role of manufacturing in the economy and coal in electricity generation

According to the environmental performance index jointly produced by Yale and Columbia universities, Czechia ranked 15th in overall environmental performance among the EU-27 countries and 19th out of the 180 countries covered by the index in 2022.[1] While between 2010 and 2020 Czechia grew by 5.2 percentage points in the overall ranking and improved in most of the specific environmental indicators composing the index, it also experienced a deterioration in the growth rate of greenhouse gas (GHG) emissions.

An important barrier to industry decarbonisation in Czechia consists in the high share of energy-intensive industries compared to the EU average, which contributes to making the national economy particularly reliant on fossil fuels. In particular, coal, Czechia's largest source of energy, still accounts for 28% of total energy supply and for 59% of total carbon-dioxide emissions from fuel combustion.[2] As a result, Czechia has the 3rd highest carbon-emission intensity (i.e., carbon emissions per capita) at the EU level (Figure 7.1), while the share of renewable energy sources (RES) in the final gross energy consumption was only 18% in 2022, up from 11% in 2010, but still behind the EU average of 23% in 2022[3] (MIT, 2024[1]). Similarly, despite a regular decrease in material intensity (i.e., the amount of material used per unit of output) since 2000, Czechia lags behind the EU average in key circular-economy (ManpowerGorup, 2024[2]) indicators such as resource productivity and the use rate of circular material (OECD, 2021[3])[4].

Figure 7.1. Carbon emission intensity of GDP, Czechia and the EU-27, 2013-2022

Adjusted for inflation (chain-linked volumes)

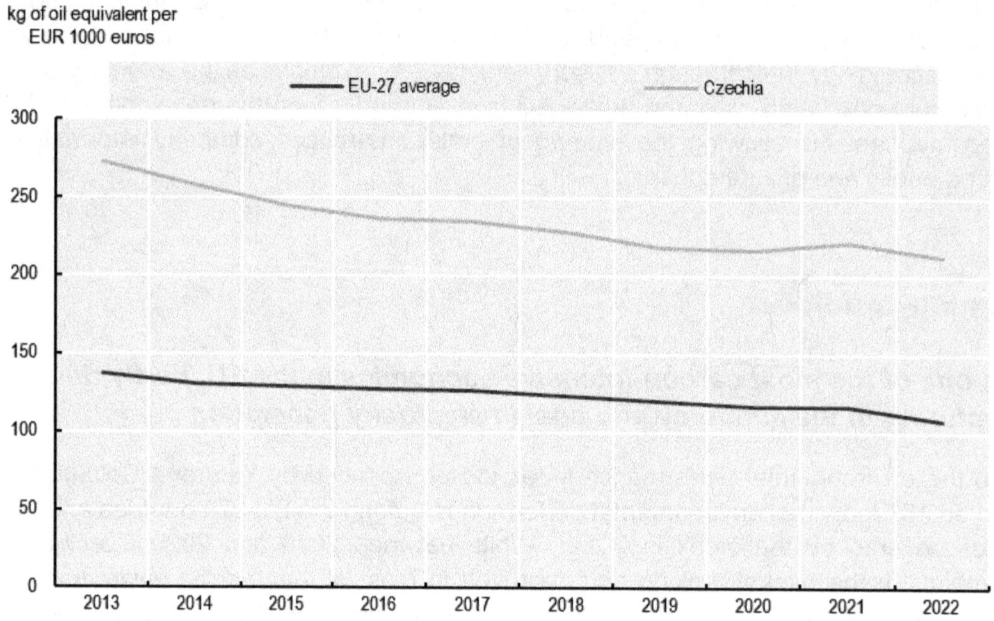

Source: OECD based on Eurostat Energy Statistics Database

Czechia continues to have a relatively high share of polluting jobs, but green-tasked jobs are on the rise

The OECD defines green jobs following a "task-based approach", whereby these are jobs that align with environmental goals or that necessitate green skills, rather than jobs in specific sectors or industries classified as green (OECD, 2023[4]). Based on this definition, the share of green jobs has been on the rise across many regions of Europe. Czechia is no exception, with the share of green jobs that increased across all 8 NUTS-2 regions between 2011 and 2021. Like in other EU countries, the capital region (Prague) features the highest share of green jobs in Czechia – i.e., 23%, 5 percentage points higher than the OECD average – which is the result of the large number of green-tasked jobs in sectors such as utilities, professional services and financial activities, which are more concentrated in large cities, notably capital regions (OECD, 2023[4]). On the other hand, the gradual phase-out of coal mining is reflected in the declining share of polluting jobs in the three coal regions of Czechia, with 2-3 percentage-point drops in Northeast and Moravia-Silesia. Nonetheless, the overall proportion of polluting jobs remains relatively high, around 24% at national level, which underscores the need for boosting more green-tasked jobs, especially outside the capital region of Prague (Figure 7.2).

Figure 7.2. Share of green jobs and polluting jobs by region in Czechia, 2011 and 2021

Percentage values

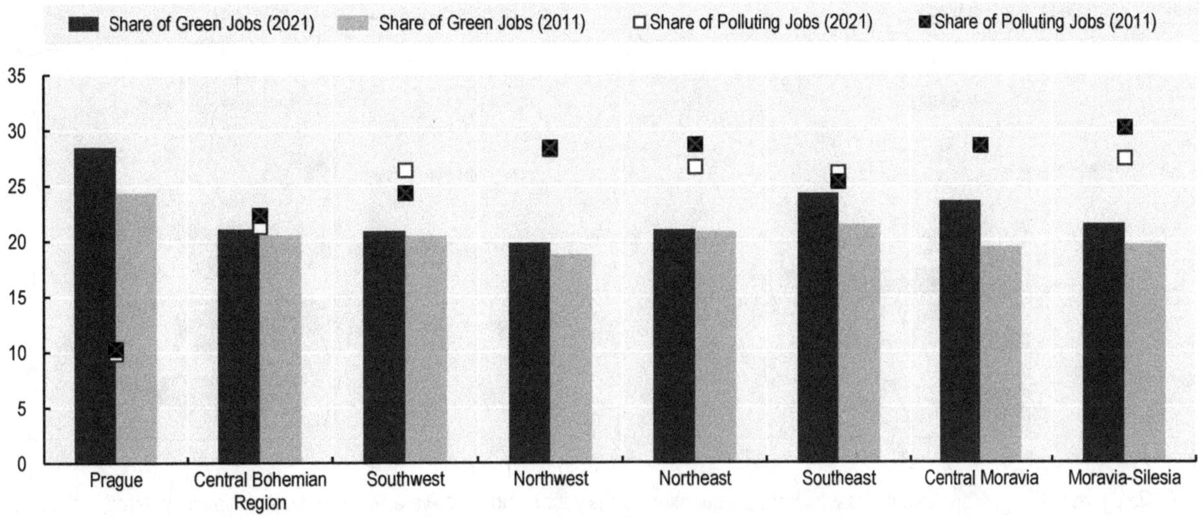

Note: The chart reflects the proportion of green jobs (occupations where at least 10% of tasks are green, or contribute to sustainability goals, whereas polluting jobs are a subset of non-green-task jobs that are particularly concentrated in high-polluting sectors).
Source: OECD based on the OECD "Job Creation and Local Economic Development 2023: Bridging the Great Green Divide" database (OECD, 2023[4]).

Additional survey evidence shows that 64% of employers in Czechia plan to recruit in green-related jobs and roles. Based on the results of this survey, at global level, the highest demand for these jobs is expected in the energy and utility sector (81% of companies), followed by manufacturing and production (36% of companies). Furthermore, other studies have pointed to labour shortages in seven technical occupations requiring specific green skills[5] in Czechia, including electrical technicians and pipefitters (EURES, 2023[5]).

Czech SMEs trails behind the EU average in the green transition

According to OECD estimates, SMEs in Czechia accounted for around 41%-48% of business-sector GHG emissions in 2018, depending on the type of sector weights used (output or employment-based), which is only marginally higher than the EU average (OECD, 2023[6]).

To reduce carbon emissions, it is helpful for SMEs to have climate neutrality strategies in place that can steer environmental actions in a more systemic way. However, based on recent Eurobarometer survey evidence, only 14% of Czech SMEs already had a climate neutrality strategy in place in 2024, compared with 21% at the EU level. Furthermore, 66% of Czech SMEs did not have such a strategy and were not planning to have one in the following two years, which is also higher than the EU average (52%). On the upside, Czech SMEs that have a climate-neutrality strategy appear to be more likely to take more concrete environmental measures, such as developing (58%) or purchasing new technologies (66%), compared with the respective EU averages (Figure 7.3). This suggests that only a small group of Czech SMEs are taking actions to reduce GHG emissions, while the majority either faces significant barriers or is reluctant to invest in the green transition.

Figure 7.3. Climate strategies and climate actions of Czech SME, 2024

Percentage values

Panel A: Climate strategy in place	Panel B: Actions towards climate neutrality

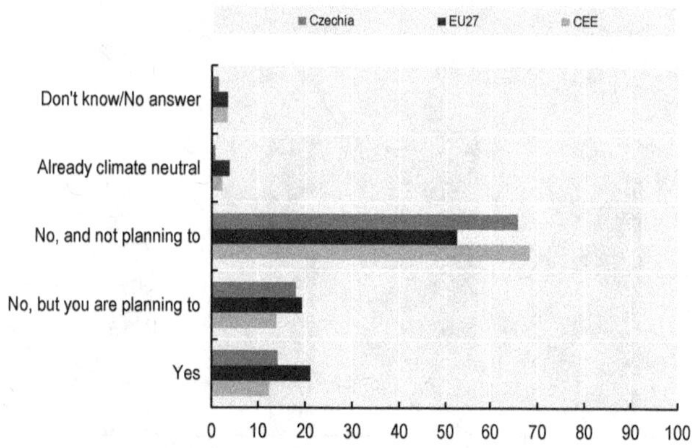

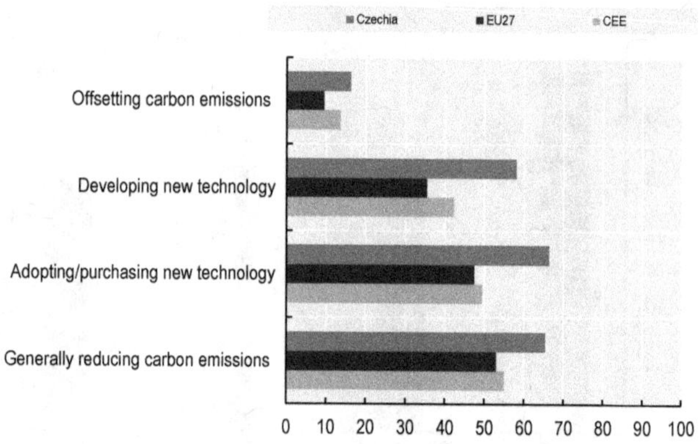

Note: The figure in Panel A displays the results from the question "Does your company have a concrete strategy in place to reduce your carbon footprint and become climate neutral or negative?". The follow-up question "What actions is your company undertaking to become climate neutral?" (Panel B) was only asked to respondents who answered "Yes" to having a climate strategy in place (see Panel A). Results are based on the 2024 Eurobarometer flash survey (FL549), conducted by the European Commission, on "SMEs, Resource Efficiency and Green Markets". The benchmark group CEE refers to the average of the countries Poland, Hungary and the Slovak Republic.
Source: OECD based on "Flash Eurobarometer FL549: SMEs, resource efficiency and green markets" (EC, 2024[7]).

Resource efficiency – which includes efficiency in the use of energy, natural resources, and materials – is a key channel through which businesses can reduce their environmental footprint. A disaggregated analysis by firm size shows that, expectedly, Czech micro (1-9 employees) and small firms (10-49 employees) are less likely than mid-sized companies (50-249 employees) to undertake resource-efficiency actions. While 89% of the latter takes at least some action in this field, only 82% of small and 75% of micro firms do the same. Despite a rising share of micro and small firms taking many actions – respectively from 40% to 48% and from 43% to 56% between 2021 and 2024 – high upfront costs, limited economies of scale, and uncertain returns on investment remain a significant barrier to resource-efficiency actions for these firms (Figure 7.4, Panel A).

There are also strong differences in resource-efficiency actions across sectors (see Figure 7.4, Panel B), with manufacturing (61%) and industry-based (53%) SMEs leading the way, followed by retail trade (50%) and services (39%). This is in line with recent OECD findings across 15 countries suggesting that SMEs in more polluting sectors, such energy-intensive manufacturing, tend to be more likely to report on their greening efforts, as they have more opportunities to take action to offset their emissions (Wildnerova et al., 2024[8]).

Figure 7.4. Resource efficiency actions by firm size (SMEs) and sector in Czechia, 2024

Percentage values

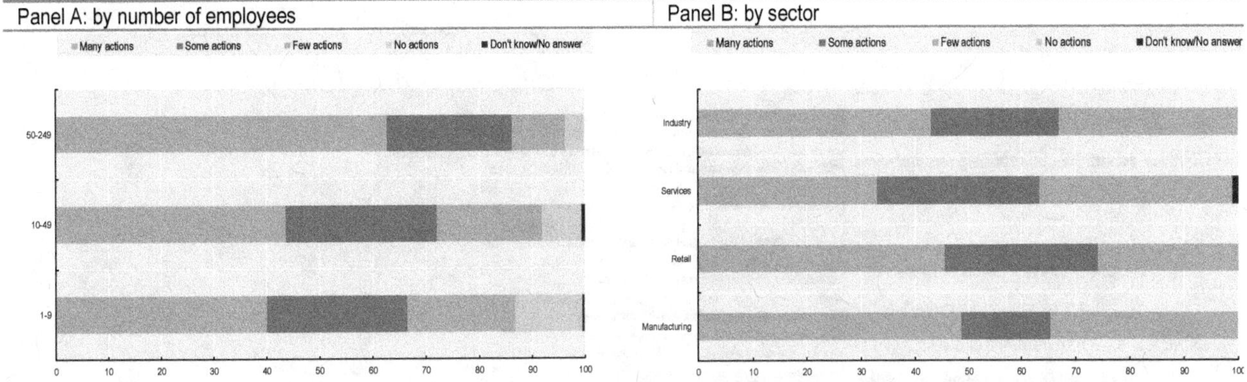

Note: The figure displays the results from the questions "What actions is your company undertaking to be more resource efficient?" from the 2024 survey. The questions were asked to all responders to the survey. For the question, it was possible to provide multiple answer alternatives, but presented here is a grouping of the responses: "many actions" = 5 or more actions, "some actions" = 3-4 actions. "few actions" = 1-2 actions, and "no actions" = 0 actions.

Firm size categories of SMEs are defined by number of employees: Micro=1-9, Small=10-49, Medium-sized= 50-249 employees.

Sectors are defined following NACE Rev.2, with "Services" representing the aggregate of "Transportation and storage (H)", "Accommodation and food service activities (I)", "Information and communication (J)", "Financial and insurance activities (K)", "Real estate activities (L)", "Professional, scientific and technical activities (M)", and "Industry" representing the aggregate of "Mining and quarrying (B)", "Electricity, gas, steam and air conditioning supply (D)", "Water supply; sewerage, waste management and remediation activities (E)", "Construction (F)".

Source: OECD based on "Flash Eurobarometer FL549: SMEs, resource efficiency and green markets" (EC, 2024[7]).

The main barriers to undertaking resource-efficiency actions reported by Czech SMEs are the complexity of administrative and legal procedures (49%), followed by the emerging challenge of complex environmental reporting requirements (34%) and the high costs of environmental actions (26%) (see Figure 7.5). On the upside, while 30% of Czech SMEs reported problems in the supply of materials, parts, products, or services in 2021, this proportion dropped to 22% in 2024, which is partly the result of the lingering effects of the Covid-19 crisis generating supply-chain disruptions in 2021 but may also point to the recent development of new national green markets.

Figure 7.5. SME barriers to resource efficiency actions, Czechia, EU and CEE, 2024

Percentage values

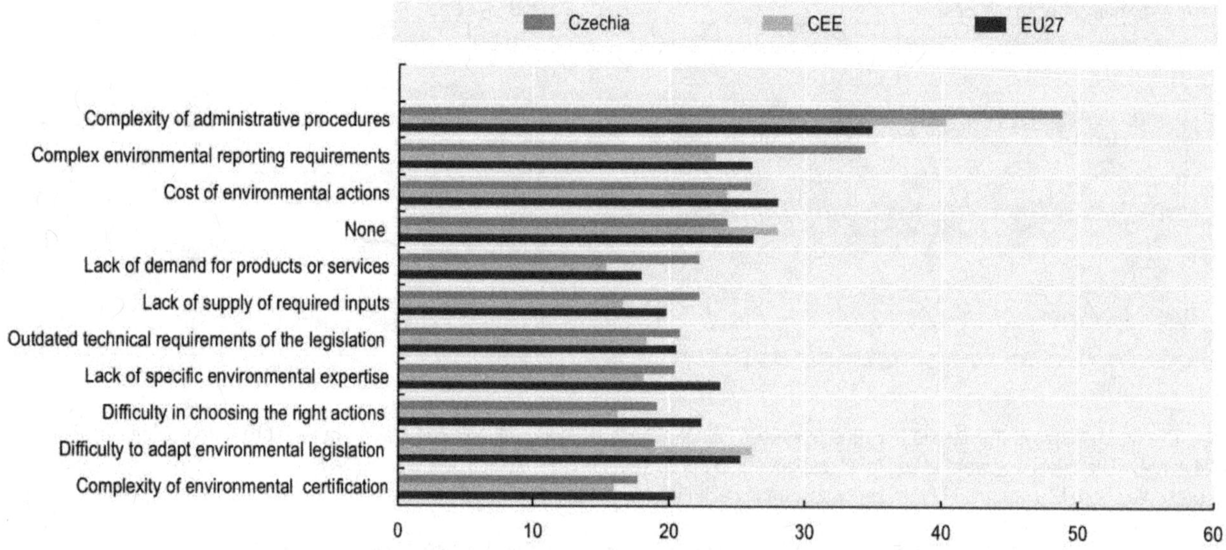

Note: The figure displays the results from the question "Did your company encounter any of the following difficulties when trying to set up resource efficiency actions?" from the 2024 survey. The question was asked only to those responding that they are taking action to the question "What actions is your company undertaking to be more resource efficient?". For the question, it was possible to provide multiple answer alternatives. The benchmark group CEE refers to the average of the countries Poland, Hungary and the Slovak Republic.
Source: OECD based on "Flash Eurobarometer FL549: SMEs, resource efficiency and green markets" (EC, 2024[7]).

Given existing barriers, external support to undertake resource-efficiency actions is key. In 2024, only 18% of Czech SMEs used external support to undertake resource-efficiency actions, which is two percentage points below the 2021 figure (20%) and below the 2024 EU average (23%). Among the Czech companies that received support, 86% received it from the private sector (EU average, 77%) and 62% from the public sector (EU average, 49%). EU-funded programmes, such as the Operational Programme Technologies and Application for Competitiveness (OP TAC) and the national Recovery and Resilience Plan (RRP), which are discussed in the following section of the chapter, help explain the larger proportion of Czech SMEs that received public support for resource efficiency actions compared with the EU average.

SME greening policies: Mid-term evaluation of the national SME Strategy

There are strong financial incentives for Czech SMEs to invest in energy efficiency

Both the national RRP and OP TAC, which is the operational programme managed by Czechia's Ministry of Industry and Trade (MIT) and financed through the European Regional Development Fund (ERDF), actively support resource-efficiency actions at firm level, including in SMEs[6]. The main programme in this field is funded through an OP TAC call named "Energy Savings". The first edition of the call, which run between 2022 and 2023, had a budget allocation of CZK 10 billion, while the second in 2024 received an allocation of CZK 5 billion. All companies, regardless of size and sector but with the exception of those based in Prague[7], can apply for grants disbursed through this programme, which cover between 35% and 80% of the energy-efficiency investment depending on the action and the size and sector of the supported company.

Eligible activities are broad and include improvements in building-related energy efficiency (e.g. better insulation or ventilation, improved electricity systems, etc.); the use of renewable energy sources (e.g. solar panels); gas, heat, and compressed air distribution systems; capture and re-use of energy waste; production modernisation; and energy management support. Furthermore, companies receiving grant support need to work with an energy expert from a database managed by the MIT, which helps to improve the effectiveness of this policy and to keep up a network of energy experts. The MIT monitors this policy by collecting information from beneficiary companies on the reduction of final energy consumption and primary energy consumption before and after project implementation. [8] In the first call, which closed in 2023, the programme supported 756 projects, three-quarters of which were run by SMEs, despite the relatively complex application and documentation requirements.

In this regard, an evaluation of a similar scheme run under the previous Operational Programme "Enterprise and Innovation for Competitiveness" (OP EIC), which was the predecessor of OP TAC covering the period 2014-2020, found that the measure had supported energy efficiency improvements affecting both production and building management, with most recipient companies reporting a decrease in energy consumption between 10-50% within a year. However, half of the programme beneficiaries also reported that they would have introduced the energy-efficiency improvements regardless of government support, pointing to the possible low additionality of this policy (MIT, 2023[9]).

More generally, while collecting information on energy consumption before and after the intervention is certainly useful, this metric cannot simply be used to assess programme effectiveness, since energy consumption can increase or decrease for reasons beyond efficiency improvements (e.g., increased production levels, global energy prices, national energy subsidies, etc.).

Moreover, while effects on energy consumption have been largely positive, there is wide variation in the energy savings rate (between 10-50%), which can depend on the sector of intervention – i.e., the scope for energy savings are larger in energy-intensive sectors – but may also point to strong heterogeneity in the energy-saving potential of the supported actions. This issue could partly be redressed through improved ex-ante analysis of the energy-saving potential of the financed projects.

Finally, low additionality may suggest that many actions have been directed at low-hanging fruits involving low-cost investments (e.g., smart lighting). This issue could be tackled through the funding of bigger-ticket investments (e.g. supporting production-related energy-efficiency investments), although self-reported feedback always needs to be taken with a grain of salt, as there is no real guarantee that respondents would have really undertaken the investment without government support, even when they say so.

Some energy-efficiency programmes target specific regions and sectors

The capital region of Prague, due to its average per-capita income, does not qualify for ERDF funding. Czechia's national development bank (NRB) has, therefore, launched a programme similar to OP TAC's Energy Savings programme, but only targeted to Prague-based businesses. The scheme (ENERG) offers interest-free loans to finance energy-efficiency investments similar to those funded under the OP TAC scheme.[9] Furthermore, the NRB offers subsidised loans to companies outside Prague under another Energy Savings programme, but loans must be co-financed by a commercial bank in this case.

The NRB also offers specific support to SMEs in three regions of Czechia with a tradition in coal-based industries (Moravian-Silesian, Ústí nad Labem and Karlovy Vary), notably through so-called Transformation Loans, which are interest-free loans funded through the EU Just Transition Fund (CZK 2 billion). The scheme assists companies, including SMEs, with the purchase of machinery and equipment, building upgrades, and the acquisition of technology licenses and software across different sectors. Loans are interest-free, the repayment period is over 10 years, and projects worth between CZK 500 000 and 100 million can be funded, with only 10% of these costs to be borne by the beneficiary. As of June 2024, 88 projects had been approved with an average loan size of CZK 6 million (i.e., about EUR 236 000), suggesting that the programme has mostly funded mid-sized investments. The take up has been stronger in two of the three targeted regions, suggesting that stronger outreach efforts may be needed in the third region.

Finally, particularly relevant to small industrial companies is the scheme “ENERG ETS: Modernisation of Sources and Technologies: Small Projects”, which has a budget of CZK 5 billion from the Modernisation Fund and is financed through the emission allowances collected through the EU ETS system. The scheme offers grants for investments in the reduction of production-related energy consumption and greenhouse gas emissions.

Overall, these measures have the merit of targeting specific regions or sectors which are in special need of support and complement the main energy saving programme run by OP TAC (see previous section). The NRB programme in Prague, for example, fills a policy gap caused by the ERDF classification of Prague as a high-income region. However, the Prague region is the economic powerhouse of the country and continues to have an important manufacturing sector, which makes its involvement in industrial decarbonisation policies still very crucial. In a similar vein, the ETS-funded measure targets energy-intensive industrial SMEs that have a large decarbonisation potential, thus warranting special attention by policymakers.

SMEs also benefit from a strong national network of energy advisors

In addition to financial support, Czech businesses (and households) also benefit from a strong network of energy advisory services. In particular, the Energy Consulting and Information Centre (EKIS) Network consists of around 50 centres that provide free advice on energy efficiency to households and businesses. In 2022, the EKIS centres conducted 10 000 consulting activities, also thanks to their mobile units (M-EKIS). EKIS funding comes from the national Programme on the Promotion of Energy Savings and the Utilisation of Renewable Energy Sources (EFEKT), which makes possible the offer of advisory services fully free for clients. Energy advisors are certified by MIT, based on technical education, two years of work experience, and an entry exam. As of 2024, there were around 1 300 certified energy experts, organised in 4 groups: a) energy audit and assessment (around 500 specialists); b) control of air conditioning; c) control of heating; d) building energy performance. Efforts are currently underway to categorise professions in energy consulting to ensure easier accessibility for clients based on their specific needs.

The MIT also runs a programme called “Energy coordinators of Local Action Groups” (EnKo MAS), which offers free energy advice to businesses and households at local level. In particular, the programme, running between 2022 and 2024 with a small budget of CZK 10.5 million (i.e., about EUR 400 000), intends to inform the public about existing energy-saving measures and available financial support, to help co-ordinate first steps in community energy projects and, more generally, to raise awareness on the importance of energy savings.

Finally, in 2024, under the National Reform Programme (NRP)[10], Czechia established three regional unified contact points to provide households, businesses, and the public sector with advice on energy-efficient renovations. Through an allocation of CZK 4 billion a system has been established to provide advisory and awareness-raising activities in the areas of sustainable projects, building renovations, the use of renewable energy sources (RES), and community energy projects, aiming to offer 120 000 advisory services by June 2026 (Government Office of the Czech Republic, 2024[10]) (EC, 2023[11]). As part of this programme, the MIT has developed a business-dedicated website that offers energy advice and information on existing investment support. Additionally, as part of the RRP and in line with the National Recovery Plan, a reform of the advisory system is underway to establish a network of one-stop shops for energy advice.

On the whole, non-financial support for energy efficiency is well developed in Czechia, although existing programmes have very similar objectives, which could undermine their cost-effectiveness and make it difficult for SMEs to discern the nuances between the different offers. Furthermore, there is a limited follow-up of the actions taken at firm level after the received advice, which makes an impact assessment of these programmes difficult. As will be seen in the next section, this problem also extends to the national energy audit system.

The national energy auditing system should be revamped

Since 2000, in line with EU legislation, Czechia has made energy audits mandatory every four years for energy-intensive companies with annual energy consumption levels above MWh 5 000 (IEECP, 2023[12]). Until recently, based on EU legislation, energy audits were voluntary for SMEs (i.e., enterprises with fewer than 250 workers and annual turnover below EUR 50 million). However, the European Commission's new Energy Efficiency Directive (EED) (2023/1791) has introduced a change in the criterion used to establish which companies are subject to an energy audit obligation, from employment size to energy consumption levels. Notably, this directive has lowered the I energy-consumption threshold to 10 terajoule (TJ) (i.e., about 2 800 MWh), regardless of the number of workers employed by the company. This change will extend the audit obligation to a larger number of SMEs, making this policy more relevant for this business segment. As of March 2025, the Czech Senate was discussing the transposition of the new EED into national legislation, including Article 11 on energy management systems and energy audits.

At present, based on information gathered during the fact-finding mission of the project, Czechia lacks a monitoring system of its energy audits. Companies required by the national law to go through an energy audit do so, but there is no follow-up to monitor if any energy-efficiency action is introduced following the audit, which undermines the effectiveness of this policy. Typically, companies, after an energy audit, are required to undertake specific actions to improve their energy efficiency, which can be encouraged through fiscal and financial incentives, such as exemptions on energy-related taxes (e.g., excise duties) or subsidised loans and grants. These benefits are often conditional on the submission of progress reports on the energy-savings measures that have effectively been implemented. Even in comprehensive national energy-audit systems, only about half of the energy efficiency measures recommended in the audits are generally implemented (Anderson and Newell, 2004[13]). This ratio is likely to drop even further in the absence of proper follow-up and enforcement, like in Czechia.

Czechia's national energy audit system would, therefore, benefit from an overhaul. First, it would be important that energy audits be followed by rationalisation plans, setting out the main energy-saving actions that audited companies are expected to undertake, including the estimated payback period for each of these actions. Second, information from energy audits could feed into an information management system, where information on energy consumption by firm size and sector and on estimated energy savings from specific measures could be collected, aggregated, and used to design better evidence-based policies (see Box 7.1 for ongoing data collection efforts in Czechia which could be complemented with this approach).

Box 7.1. Czechia's Energy Performance Database

A new information system, called "Energy Performance Database" (DEN), is currently under development in Czechia. It will serve as a tool both to monitor the registration of energy professionals and their activities and the energy performance of buildings. It will replace the existing system which has so far only managed the agenda and training of energy specialists. Through its integration with the building database, the new system is expected to document the renovation of public buildings in compliance with the new EU EED and to integrate data from voluntary agreements.

Building on data from enterprise energy audits, it would also be useful to include in this new database detailed information on energy consumption by firm size and sector and on the impact of selected energy-savings measures, including payback periods. By collecting and aggregating these data, the government would have a better understanding of the average enterprise energy performance by sector and firm size, which will support the policymaking process, while energy auditors would benefit from this repository of knowledge in their auditing work.

Additional future reforms of the national energy audit system could include the integration of international standards in energy management system as part of the auditing process (see also below) and the extension of energy audits to less energy-intensive SMEs on a voluntary basis. The first policy would ensure that energy audits go beyond advice on production or support-systems (e.g., lighting, ventilation, etc.) to embrace a holistic understanding of how energy can be managed at firm level (e.g., analysis of consumption peaks during the day and the year, analysis of energy costs during the day, etc.). The second policy would enable smaller SMEs to better understand the importance of energy use and energy management for their business and offer concrete advice on possible improvements. Suggested actions could be financially supported by the government, depending on budget availability.

Czechia could consider the launch of new targeted energy programmes

The Czech government could also consider new programmes to further encourage energy efficiency at the firm level, notably through the adoption of energy management systems and the launch of energy efficiency networks.

In 2024, Czechia only counted 328 ISO 50001 certificates (i.e., the reference international standard in energy management systems), compared with above 10 000 in Germany.[11] Voluntary Agreement Programmes (VAPs) can foster the adoption of energy management systems (EnMS) in large energy-intensive companies through the offer of tax breaks and other financial incentives on condition that energy-savings targets are met. These programmes combine an energy audit with management and workforce training supporting compliance with an international EnMS standard (e.g., on software to better manage energy consumption and good practices to improve energy savings).

Energy efficiency networks are more relevant to SMEs, especially in light industries. They involve regular meetings of SME business owners or managers, preferably from the same sector or related sectors, over a period of 3-4 years. Meetings and other activities are co-ordinated and steered by an expert, who help network members to identify energy-efficient solutions and/or to pool resources towards joint investments.

There has been progress in the uptake of renewable energy sources by SMEs, whereas SME participation in renewable energy industries is limited

In addition to energy efficiency, the Government of Czechia has also encouraged the adoption of renewable energy sources (RES) by SMEs. The main programme in this area has been a call, launched by the MIT in 2022 with a budget of CZK 1 billion from the national RRP, to encourage the installation of solar panels by SMEs, also in combination with batteries. The project received strong interest from SMEs, with 5 000 approved projects, and facilitated an estimated 270 MWh of added photovoltaic capacity, corresponding to a 14% progress towards the 2030 objective[12]. Besides financial support measures, the government of Czechia has also increased the threshold for renewable-energy production without a license, from a maximum output of 10 kWh to 50kWh, which is expected to facilitate the generation of renewable energy by SMEs in the future.

A small number of SMEs with the license to operate in the energy sector have also participated in the larger RES+ call, which received CZK 4 billion funding from the Modernisation Fund in 2022. The call has supported projects in renewable-energy industries and technologies such as photovoltaics, biomethane, hydroelectric plants and wind farms, some of which typically require large upfront investments. Support was provided in the form of a one-off ex post subsidy paid after submitting documents proving the completed implementation of the project. SMEs benefitted from preferential conditions in the form of a 10% (for medium-sized enterprises) and 20% (for small enterprises) of additional investment aid for the outlined projects (State Environmental Fund of the Czech Republic, 2021[14]). Despite grant bonuses given to SMEs, few of them have benefited from this call: two respectively in wind farms and biomethane and four in hydroelectric plants.

The Czech government could encourage stronger SME participation in future RES development projects, for example, starting with the green hydrogen industry, whose national strategy was updated in 2024 with the objective of producing 20 000 tons of renewable hydrogen per year by 2030.[13] The hydrogen industry is generally led by large energy companies, as upfront investments for green hydrogen production through electrolysis are high and industry regulations are still in the making, which may further discourage small operators. Nonetheless, a recent Important Project of Common European Interest (IPCEI), funded by the European Commission through EUR 6.9 billion, is expected to finance 33 green hydrogen projects with the participation of 32 companies, including 5 SMEs, suggesting that there is scope for involving SMEs also in cutting-edge technologies like green hydrogen[14]. In particular, SMEs can be suppliers of large energy companies (e.g. of parts and components used in the electrolysis process) or play an active role in support activities like energy storage. The Czech government could support SME participation in the green hydrogen supply chain through specific calls, to be funded by a relevant operational programme, as well as through awareness-raising and training initiatives. Such an approach would ensure that hydrogen development better support job creation at local level, which is one of the objectives of the EU Strategy towards "green hydrogen valleys", i.e., local areas that promote the production and use of green hydrogen through the development of infrastructure and partnerships between industry, government, and local communities[15].

The government has fostered the uptake of electric vehicles (EVs) by SMEs, although the EV diffusion is still weak

While the EU-27 average for newly registered electric vehicles (EVs) – including battery electric vehicles (BEVs) and plug-in hybrid vehicles – stood at 18.5% in 2022, Czechia ranked second-last in the EU, with only about 4% of new vehicle registrations involving EVs[16], which is partly the result of less generous EV incentives in Czechia compared to other EU countries. As a consequence, Czechia lagged significantly behind the targets set out in the National Action Plan for Clean Mobility in 2022[17].

To make progress in this area, Czechia's MIT has supported the acquisition of EVs and charging stations by SMEs through a call under the previous operational programme OP EIC, which approved 520 projects resulting in the purchase of 826 EVs and 347 charging stations. This measure was complemented by the OP Transport 2014-2020, which further developed the network of charging stations. As highlighted in the 2024 update of the National Action Plan for Clean Mobility, a basic coverage of public charging stations (accounting for around 20% of charging needs) has been achieved across Czechia, including fast-charging stations (Czech Government, 2024[15]). However, a persistent challenge is the low average utilisation of these stations, i.e., 2% in 2022 well below Germany (8.5%), Sweden (9.5%), and Denmark (27%). While some imbalance is to be expected at the beginning, since the construction of charging infrastructure initially tends to outpace the sales of vehicles, the current major gap in Czechia suggests that there should be better co-ordination between the rollout of infrastructure (i.e., charging stations) and the market uptake (i.e., of electric vehicles) to limit overcapacity and underutilisation. Stronger incentives for the acquisition of EVs can clearly help address this imbalance.

More recently, in March 2024, through funding from the RRP (CZK 1.95 billion), Czechia's national development bank (NRB) launched the electromobility guarantee programme, which offers companies of all sizes loan guarantees for the purchase of emission-free vehicles and charging stations, as well as grant contributions up to CZK 300 000 per vehicle.[18] Since its launch, the programme has experienced high demand, with around 80% of the total budget spent in the first six months to finance the acquisition of 5 300 EVs and over 2 200 charging stations, exceeding the initial objectives of 4 055 vehicles and 1 500 charging stations.

The NRB programme has been successful, as shown by its strong uptake, but the available funding will run out very soon, which is also the consequence of the generous conditions of the scheme (i.e., up to CZK 300 000 per vehicle, i.e., about EUR 12 300). Moving forward, the generosity of similar measures could be reduced so that more companies can benefit from support, although financial incentives will still be important, as EVs remain on average 30% more expensive than equivalent fuel-burning cars.[19]

National programmes supporting circularity in SMEs should be scaled up

The promotion of the circular economy is also a priority at the EU level. In addition to reducing waste, the circular economy directly affects industry decarbonisation by reducing the need for new material and products to be manufactured. Czechia's circular economy strategy is laid out in the "Strategic Framework for the Circular Economy of the Czech Republic 2040", while specific actions are included in the "Action Plan: 2022-2027". A stronger diffusion of the circular economy is particularly relevant for Czechia, as national resource productivity – i.e., the efficiency with which material resources are used in the economy – lags behind the EU average, and Czechia's material consumption is expected to increase by one third by 2050 (OECD, 2021[3]). Furthermore, high levels of commodity prices put pressure on national budgets, further accentuating the importance of the circular economy to reduce dependency on volatile raw material prices. Against this backdrop, SMEs can play a crucial role in reducing resource consumption through the use of technologies that support the recovery, processing, and use of secondary raw materials.

The main national circular economy projects are supported by OP TAC, which is managed by the Ministry of Industry and Trade (MIT), and by the Operational Programme Environment, which is managed by the Ministry of Environment. The most relevant initiative for SMEs has been a call under OP TAC, which was budgeted with CZK 1 billion and provided grants to SMEs to support investments in better materials and re-use of production waste (54%), waste prevention (53%), technologies enabling creation of secondary raw materials (30%), eco-design, and enhanced recyclability of products (10%)[20]. Recognising the interdependency of many of these activities and technologies, the call was flexible enough to allow companies to apply for more than one type of investment at once. The call received 300 applications, about half of which (160) were approved. This can be considered a high approval rate, but it is in line with the experience of EU-funded programmes in which the programme budget needs to be spent relatively quickly. As of end-2024, a follow up of this project call was already underway and another one in the making, for a total budget of CZK 2.5 billion.

Going forward, it would be recommended to scale up circular-economy projects for SMEs in Czechia. As noted earlier, material intensity is high in Czechia and has not improved significantly in recent years: for example, between 2011 and 2018, the share in the use of secondary raw material only rose from 8% to 8.3% (Czech Environmental Information Agency, 2022[16]). In addition, the evaluation of circular economy projects under the previous operational programme of the MIT (OP EIC, 2014-2020) points to positive impacts of these measures on the increased use of secondary raw materials (MIT, 2023[9]).

Advisory services, sound legislation and adequate infrastructure should complement financial incentives to further promote the circular economy

While financial support is key, it should also be complemented with advisory services, adequate legislation and quality infrastructure to ensure that the circular economy unleash its potential. For example, the establishment of regional circular-economy hubs could further support circularity by offering tailored advisory services for SMEs and by helping them navigate relevant processes and existing funding opportunities. By facilitating multi-stakeholder dialogue (government, business associations, technology and research institutes), these hubs could act as platforms for networking and knowledge-sharing (OECD, 2020[17]). The dual approach of providing SMEs with streamlined access to expert advice while helping public actors understand the practical challenges that SMEs face to become more resource-efficient would be a key strength of these hubs. This model could draw inspiration from successful examples, such as Scotland's Circular Economy Business Support Service. Alternatively, rather than establishing entirely new hubs, the existing network of Czechia's regional innovation centers could be leveraged to deliver similar services. These centers already provide bespoke business support to SMEs and start-ups and play a critical role in co-ordinating regional innovation strategies, including those outlined in the National RIS3 strategy (see chapter 5 on R&D and innovation).

Adequate legislation and quality infrastructure are also essential to ensure that key circular-economy activities, such as eco-design and recycling, are possible and easy to perform for businesses. As noted in the first section of this chapter, "complexity of administrative procedures" is the main barrier to undertaking resource-efficiency actions in Czechia, pointing to the importance of simplifying regulations in this area. Support for recycling infrastructure, recycled products and markets for secondary materials are also important pillars for the promotion of the circular economy (OECD, 2021[3]), which take even more importance after the government's decision to discontinue preferential taxation for recycling activities[21]. Alternative mechanisms to increase demand for recycled or repaired products could include the promotion and simplification of the existing ecolabel system. Similarly, raising awareness and providing informational tools on how to share clear and accessible product details at the point of sale can also shift consumer and businesses demand for circular products (OECD, 2021[3]).

Finally, monitoring SME participation in the circular economy would provide valuable insights for policymakers. Beyond the targets of the implementation plan of the SME Support strategy, which primarily focus on the number of completed projects, there are several indicators which could offer valuable information for policymakers which could be shaped after the macro indicators used in the EU Circular Economy Monitoring Framework (OECD, 2021[3]).[22]

Box 7.2. Possible indicators to monitor SME participation in the circular economy

The following indicators could be monitored in the implementation of the national SME Strategy to assess the participation of domestic SMEs in the circular economy:

- Number of patents related to recycling – This indicator would reflect the progress of innovative SMEs in the development of new recycling technologies. Data could be gathered by the Industrial Property Office of Czechia.
- Private investments in circular innovations – This indicator would reflect the profitability and scalability of circular-economy solutions. The data could be sourced from applications for public funding or R&D tax incentives
- Circular material usage rate by SMEs – This indicator would represent the share of secondary materials used in the total input materials of SMEs. This indicator would provide insights into the integration of circular-economy practices in the business model of SMEs. While SME-specific data may not yet be available, it would be recommended to include a similar aggregate indicator for the whole business sector in the "Czechia 2040 Circular Economy Framework". As monitoring capabilities progress, this indicator could be further refined so to capture SME-specific data.

There is not yet a systemic approach to green skills development in Czechia

In the face of increasing demand for green skills, the OECD has pointed out the importance of training policies that target both high-skilled workers, for example through new university curricula, and mid- and low-skilled workers, including through on-the-job training and micro-certifications (Pissareva et al., 2025[18]).

As of mid-2024, Czechia had not yet put in place extensive green skills policies, despite the presence of three coal regions which could benefit from these programmes. The Operational Programme Just Transition (OP JT)[23], which has a budget of CZK 41 billion, has supported SMEs in these regions through advisory services, including through the offer of innovation and digital vouchers, and knowledge-sharing activities, for example informing SMEs about opportunities in the hydrogen economy in the region of Karlovy Vary. Initial feedback from SMEs suggests interest to extend the voucher programme also to cover education and professional training activities (Frankfurt School of Finance and Management, 2024[19]).

More generally, there is scope for a more systemic approach to green skills development in Czechia. For instance, there are currently no programmes that identify the needs of regional employers and provide job seekers with the specific (green) skills in demand (Shaikovski and Broughton, 2021[20]). To do so, it would be useful to monitor the offer of green skills and the distribution of green and brown jobs across the different regions of Czechia, as this would enable the identification of possible mismatches between the demand and supply of green skills at the regional level. The experience of dedicated national labour market research centre, like the one existing in France (i.e., *Observatoire national des emplois et métiers de l'économie verte*), may offer useful lessons for similar exercises in Czechia.

The Czech government should support SME sustainability reporting through advisory services and automated reporting systems

One important green skill involves sustainability reporting, i.e., the ability of companies to report on their levels of carbon emissions. One of the key pillars of the EU Corporate Sustainability Reporting Directive (CSRD), adopted in 2022, concerns the European Sustainability Reporting Standards (ESRS), which companies subject to the CSRD will need to integrate in their reporting framework from 2025. While most

European SMEs are not directly exposed to this obligation, they may have to comply with ESRS when they ask for credit or if they are suppliers of larger firms, as both financial institutions and large companies are asked by the CSRD to report respectively on the emissions of their client portfolio and on the emissions generated along their supply chains (i.e., the so-called Scope 3 emissions) (OECD, 2022[21]).

As of end-2024, the European Financial Reporting Advisory Group (EFRAG), a private association established in 2001 to provide technical advice to the European Commission on the draft of sustainability reporting standards, was working on the development of European "Voluntary Sustainability Reporting Standards" (VSME) for non-listed SMEs, whereas listed SMEs are expected in principle to comply with the same ESRS obligations as large companies. This is a welcome step, although it is not clear if VSME reporting requirements will be comprehensive enough for large companies to be able to report on Scope III emissions in the context of supply-chain relationships, as demanded by the CSRD.

While legislation in sustainability reporting requirements is mostly set at the EU level, the Czech government could support this process in at least three ways. First, it would be important that national initiatives in sustainability reporting closely align with existing EU initiatives, to ensure that SMEs are not faced with multiple and different reporting demands and standards at the same time. A harmonised approach, at least at the EU level, is key if SMEs are to comply with and benefit from sustainability reporting. Second, advisory services can help SMEs navigate a fairly complex legislation, possibly involving other key stakeholders such as the main employer associations and the regional innovation centres. A knowledge-sharing web platform could also be set-up, as done by Portugal's Knowledge Platform on ESG and Sustainable Finance. Finally, "automated reporting" can help SMEs comply with at least some of the ESG reporting requirements at low cost, although there are always data confidentiality issues to be solved when private information is shared between different actors. One example is emissions related to energy consumption, which could be calculated based on information from energy bills. The "Project Perseus", which is run by the association Bankers for Net Zero in the United Kingdom, offers an example of this approach.[24]

Box 7.3. SME greening policies from an EU legislation perspective

The EU's main energy efficiency legislation, the Energy Efficiency Directive (EED), sets rules and obligations for EU countries to meet energy-saving targets. First adopted in 2012 and revised in 2018 and 2023, the latest update (EU/2023/1791) introduces the "energy-efficiency-first" principle and a target of reducing energy consumption by 11.7% by 2030. Czechia's SME Support Strategy is broadly aligned with the revised EED through a number of energy-efficiency programmes offering both financing and advisory services. However, as seen earlier, the national energy audit system could be reformed to ensure that audits are followed by the implementation of concrete energy-efficiency measures, notably through the draft of energy rationalisation plans and the offer of incentives to implement the measures suggested in these plans. This will allow to increase the contribution of energy audits to national energy-savings targets, which is currently set at only 3 000 Terajoules, i.e., 0.5% of the total. In this regard, the major energy-savings contributions from the business sector are expected from the Modernisation Fund (i.e., 80 000 Terajoules, which is about 12% of the total energy-savings targets).

Czechia also promotes renewable energy among SMEs in line with its national target of achieving a 30% renewable-energy share by 2030 (National Energy and Climate Plan). Strong uptake of MIT's solar installation schemes and streamlined permitting for small energy producers are contributing to this goal. However, the EU has raised the 2030 renewable-energy target to at least 42.5% under the revised Renewable Energy Directive (EU/2023/2413). This implies increasing Czechia's national target to 33%.

While legislation is pending, meeting the new goal will require intensified efforts both in terms of infrastructure development and increased uptake by households and businesses, including SMEs.

Finally, the EU's Circular Economy Action Plan (CEAP), a core element of the Green Deal, promotes waste prevention and circular practices across many sectors, including some with strong SME participation (e.g., packaging, plastics and textiles). Czechia's circular-economy support programmes are well aligned with CEAP by supporting improved use of materials, re-use of production waste, waste prevention, and product eco-design, but they are relatively modest in size given the strong material intensity of the Czech economy. As noted earlier, complementary measures would be needed to make further strides in the promotion of the circular economy in the SME population.

Conclusions and policy recommendations

In recent years, Czechia has made considerable progress in decarbonising its economy, although it remains one of the most energy-intensive countries in the EU, which is partly linked to its industry composition, notably the relatively large weight of manufacturing. SMEs account for between 41% and 48% of GHG emissions, similar to the EU average, but face significant challenges in the implementation of resource-efficiency actions. Nonetheless, Czech SMEs that have adopted climate strategies are also somewhat pro-active in the adoption of specific green technologies.

The Czech government has introduced various financial and advisory programmes to foster the green transition of SMEs, notably through EU funding sources such as the European Regional Development Fund (ERDF), the Recovery and Resilience Facility, the Modernisation Fund, and the Just Transition Fund. Priority has been placed on financial incentives for energy efficiency and the uptake of renewable energy sources at the firm level. Czechia also benefits from a good network of energy efficiency advisors, while the national energy audit systems could be reformed to better contribute to the national energy-savings targets.

Areas where the government could invest more, on the other hand, include the circular economy, green skills, and supporting compliance with sustainability reporting requirements. Current circular economy programmes are relatively small given the size of the challenge – i.e., the high material intensity of the Czech economy – while green skills policies are still undeveloped despite the possibility of using funding from the Just Transition Fund for this purpose, especially in the three coal-mining regions of Czechia (i.e., Usti, Moravian-Silesian and Karlovy Vary). Finally, the Czech government could ease SME compliance with sustainability reporting requirements through advisory services and "automated" reporting mechanisms, by which relevant information on the carbon emissions of business enterprises could be shared between authorised public and private entities.

Against this backdrop, the following recommendations are put forward to enhance the green transition of SMEs in Czechia:

- Reform the national energy audit system to ensure compliance with Article 11 of the new EU Energy Efficiency Directive, which extends the audit obligation to all companies with annual energy consumption above 10 Terajoules. In this regard, consider the introduction of financial incentives for SMEs going through an energy audit to help them implement the energy savings measures suggested by the auditors.
- Establish an energy information system that builds on data stemming from the energy audits and presents aggregate information energy consumption by sector and firm size and on the average payback period of main energy-savings measures.
- Streamline the current offer of energy advisory services with a view to creating one flagship programme with a bigger budget and better visibility to the SME targeted audience.

- Continue encouraging the uptake of renewable energy sources by SMEs (e.g., solar panels), while also fostering more active participation by domestic SMEs in green supply chains, such as in the green hydrogen valleys.
- Scale up the existing offer of financial incentives for the adoption of circular-economy business models and complement such offer with new advisory services and adequate recycling infrastructure. In this respect, consider the creation of Regional Circular Economy Hubs, a role which could also be performed by the existing regional innovation centres.
- Invest in green skills policies through programmes that target both high-skilled workers (e.g. through university courses) and mid- and low-skilled workers (e.g., through on-the-job training and micro-certifications). The Operational Programme "Just Transition" could be leveraged to this aim.
- Monitor labour market trends, including new job demands in green industries and tasks, to ensure that the demand for green skills is met by the training offer.
- Introduce advisory services and experiment with an "automated" information-sharing mechanisms to help SMEs comply with sustainability reporting requirements.

References

Anderson, S. and R. Newell (2004), "Information programs for technology adoption: the case of energy-efficiency audits", *Resource and Energy Economics*, Vol. 26/1, pp. 27-50, https://doi.org/10.1016/j.reseneeco.2003.07.001. [13]

Czech Environmental Information Agency (2022), *Report on the Environment of the Czech Republic 2022*, https://www.cenia.cz/publikace/zpravy-o-zp/. [16]

Czech Government (2024), *Update of the National Action Plan for Clean Mobility (NAP CM)*, https://www.mpo.gov.cz/en/guidepost/for-the-media/press-releases/clean-and-sustainable-transport--government-approves-the-update-to-the-national-action-plan-for-clean-mobility---282798/. [15]

EC (2024), *Flash Eurobarometer FL498 : SMEs, resource efficiency and green markets*, https://data.europa.eu/data/datasets/s3221_fl549_eng?locale=en. [7]

EC (2023), *Analysis of the recovery and resilience plan of Czechia - Accompanying the document*, https://eur-lex.europa.eu/legal-content/EN/TXT/HTML/?uri=CELEX%3A52023SC0319. [11]

EURES (2023), *Report on labour shortages and surpluses*, https://www.ela.europa.eu/sites/default/files/2024-05/EURES-Shortages_Report-V8.pdf. [5]

Frankfurt School of Finance and Management (2024), *Support to the implementation of the Just Transition in the Czech Republic*, https://mmr.gov.cz/getmedia/0e1c01f1-5a3f-43ac-a6d7-2f429237378d/D3-Documentation-for-application-to-the-JTF-under-the-groups-of-projects-_JT-CZ_Final_EN-for-publication.pdf.aspx?ext=.pdf. [19]

Government Office of the Czech Republic (2024), *National Reform Programme of the Czech Republic 2024*, https://vlada.gov.cz/assets/evropske-zalezitosti/aktualne/NPR-2024_EN-version_2.pdf. [10]

IEECP (2023), *Overview of energy audit obligations across Europe – Comparing energy audit requirements from 6 EU countries*, https://ieecp.org/publications/overview-of-energy-audit-obligations-across-europe-comparing-energy-audit-requirements-from-6-eu-countries/. [12]

ManpowerGorup (2024), *Building Competitive Advantage with A People-First Green Business Transformation*, https://www.manpowergroup.cz/green-business-transformation/. [2]

MIT (2024), *Podíl obnovitelných zdrojů energie na hrubé konečné spotřebě energie 2010-2020*, https://www.mpo.gov.cz/assets/cz/energetika/statistika/obnovitelne-zdroje-energie/2024/3/SHARES-2010-2022.pdf. [1]

MIT (2023), *Ex-post evaluation of OP PIK and replication of the counterfactual impact evaluation of OP PI – Final report.* [9]

OECD (2023), "Assessing greenhouse gas emissions and energy consumption in SMEs: Towards a pilot dashboard of SME greening and green entrepreneurship indicators", *OECD SME and Entrepreneurship Papers*, No. 42, OECD Publishing, Paris, https://doi.org/10.1787/ac8e6450-en. [6]

OECD (2023), *Job Creation and Local Economic Development 2023: Bridging the Great Green Divide*, OECD Publishing, Paris, https://doi.org/10.1787/21db61c1-en. [4]

OECD (2022), "Financing SMEs for sustainability: Drivers, Constraints and Policies", *OECD SME and Entrepreneurship Papers*, No. 35, OECD Publishing, Paris, https://doi.org/10.1787/a5e94d92-en. [21]

OECD (2021), "Towards a national strategic framework for the circular economy in the Czech Republic: Analysis and a proposed set of key elements", *OECD Environment Policy Papers*, No. 27, OECD Publishing, Paris, https://doi.org/10.1787/5d33734d-en. [3]

OECD (2020), *The Circular Economy in Cities and Regions: Synthesis Report*, OECD Urban Studies, OECD Publishing, Paris, https://doi.org/10.1787/10ac6ae4-en. [17]

Pissareva, L. et al. (2025), "Equipping SMEs with the skills to navigate the twin transition", *OECD SME and Entrepreneurship Papers*, No. 65, OECD Publishing, Paris, https://doi.org/10.1787/caf420e6-en. [18]

Shaikovski, M. and A. Broughton (2021), *Marie Shaikovski and Andrea Broughton,*, EC, https://energy.ec.europa.eu/system/files/2021-06/employment_and_skills_in_karlovy_vary_-_part_ii_0.pdf. [20]

State Environmental Fund of the Czech Republic (2021), *Programme for the provision of support from the Modernisation Fund: New Renewable Energy Sources (RES+)*, https://www.sfzp.cz/files/documents/storage/2021/05/20/1621500994_ModF_RES_EN.pdf. [14]

Wildnerova, L. et al. (2024), "Which SMEs are greening?: Cross-country evidence from one million websites", *OECD SME and Entrepreneurship Papers*, No. 60, OECD Publishing, Paris, https://doi.org/10.1787/ddd00999-en. [8]

Notes

[1] The Environmental Performance Index (EPI) ranks a total of 180 countries according to their efforts in the policy goals of Environmental Health, Enhancing Ecosystem Vitality and Climate Policy. The overall EPI summarises the state of sustainable development and shows which countries are responding best to current environmental challenges. For further information: https://www.cenia.cz/publikace/monografie/slozity-svet-jednim-cislem/ .

[2] Total energy supply is the total energy available in a country, including production and imports minus exports and storage, encompassing energy used directly or transformed for consumption. Further information on GHG emissions and energy use in Czechia is available at the following websites: https://www.iea.org/countries/czechia/emissions and https://www.iea.org/countries/czechia/energy-mix .

[3] Data from: https://ec.europa.eu/eurostat/statistics-explained/index.php?title=Renewable_energy_statistics#:~:text=The%20EU%20reached%20a%2023.0,pp)%20higher%20than%20in%202021.

[4] Material intensity is measured as Domestic Material Consumption over GDP. Resource productivity measures the efficiency with which the economy uses material resources to produce wealth; it is the inverse of material intensity. Resource productivity in Czechia was equal to EUR 1.2 per kg in 2018, versus the EU average of EUR 2.24 per kg. Circular material use rate in Czechia was equal to 8.1% in 2017, versus the EU average of 11.7%. Additional information at OECD (2021[3]), “Towards a national strategic framework for the circular economy in the Czech Republic: Analysis and a proposed set of key elements”, *OECD Environment Policy Papers*, No. 27, OECD Publishing, Paris, https://doi.org/10.1787/5d33734d-en.

[5] Green skills are defined in this case as “the knowledge, abilities, values and attitudes needed to live in, develop and support a sustainable and resource-efficient society”. Further information is available at: OECD (2023[4]), *Job Creation and Local Economic Development 2023: Bridging the Great Green Divide*, OECD Publishing, Paris, https://doi.org/10.1787/21db61c1-en.

[6] At the peak of the 2022/2023 energy crisis, Czech SMEs, together with larger companies and households, benefited from electricity and gas price caps, which have kept energy prices artificially low when the cost of energy had risen to unprecedented levels. The price cap for SMEs was set at 80% of the highest consumption for the calendar month under consideration in the past five years. Additional information is available at: https://www.energiezamene.cz/strop-cen-pro-firmy. As of mid-2024, these measures were being phased out, pointing to the importance of continued progress on energy efficiency to reduce the impact of energy costs on SME profitability.

[7] The region of Prague does not qualify for ERDF support due to the average level of income per capita.

[8] Further information on the programme “Energy savings – Call II” at: https://www.agentura-api.org/cs/podporovane-aktivity-optak/uspory-energie-optak/uspory-energie-vyzva-ii/ .

[9] Further information on the ENERG programme at:: https://www.nrb.cz/en/produkt/energ/ .

[10] The National Reform Programme (NRP outlines the government’s planned reforms and key public investments for the following twelve months to address economic, social, and environmental challenges.

[11] The full ISO Survey of certifications to management system standards results (2024) is available at the ISO website: https://www.iso.org/committee/54998.html?t=KomURwikWDLiuB1P1c7SjLMLEAgXOA7emZHKGWyn8f3KQUTU3m287NxnpA3DIuxm&view=documents#section-isodocuments-top .

[12] The target value for 2030 is 3975 MWh, while the baseline value in 2018 was 2075 MWh.

[13] Further information on the national government hydrogen strategy is available at the following website: https://www.mpo.gov.cz/en/guidepost/for-the-media/press-releases/government-approved-the-update-of-the-hydrogen-strategy-of-the-czech-republic--282178/

[14] Further information at: "Commission approves up to EUR 6.9 billion of State aid by seven Member States for the third Important Project of Common European Interest in the hydrogen value chain", https://ec.europa.eu/commission/presscorner/detail/en/ip_24_789.

[15] An example of green hydrogen valley in Czechia is the H2 triangle project in the Ústí nad Labem Region, which was approved in 2022 under the Operational Programme Just Transition (https://opst.cz/projekt/h2-triangle/).

[16] Calculations based on data from the European Environment Agency (EEA) (2023), https://www.eea.europa.eu/en/analysis/indicators/new-registrations-of-electric-vehicles .

[17] Among others, the plan sets the target of at least 220 000 electric vehicles on the street by 2030.

[18] Additional information on the Electromobility programme is available at the NRB website: https://www.nrb.cz/en/entrepreneurs-and-companies-received-czk-65m-eur-2-6m-from-the-nrb-to-support-electromobility/.

[19] See: "Electric vehicle sales are stumbling. Here's why", https://www.businesstimes.com.sg/international/electric-vehicle-sales-are-stumbling-heres-why.

[20] The aid intensity in this programme was as follows: small enterprises, 60%: medium-sized enterprises, 50%; and small mid-caps, 40%. Grants ranged between CZK 1 million and CZK 100 million. Additional information at: https://www.agentura-api.org/wp-content/uploads/2023/09/obehove-hospodarstvi-vyzva-i-cs-en-gb-c.pdf.

[21] As of January 2024, the standard VAT rate of 21% applied to waste-related activities, thereby abandoning the plan for a reduced VAT rate for recycling processes.

[22] For an overview of potentially relevant indicators, see also chapter "*8. Monitoring and evaluation plan"* in OECD (2021[3]), "Towards a national strategic framework for the circular economy in the Czech Republic: Analysis and a proposed set of key elements", *OECD Environment Policy Papers*, No. 27, OECD Publishing, Paris, https://doi.org/10.1787/5d33734d-en.

[23] Additional information on the Operational Programme "Just Transition" is available at the following website: https://www.sfzp.cz/en/administered-programmes/operational-programme-just-transition/ .

[24] More information on project Perseus is available on the B4NZ website: https://www.bankersfornetzero.co.uk/perseus/.